Answered Prayers

Conversations with the Living God

Nelson P. Miller

Answered prayers: conversations with the living God.

Miller, Nelson P.

Published by:

Crown Management LLC – August 2016

1527 Pineridge Drive
Grand Haven, MI 49417
USA

ISBN: 978-0-9980601-0-1

All Rights Reserved
© 2016 Nelson P. Miller
c/o 111 Commerce Avenue S.W.
Grand Rapids, MI 49503
(616) 301-6800 ext. 6963

*Dear reader,
hush, listen:
prayer calls.*

*No, reader,
pray too, Him
hearing us
together.*

*He cares too
much for us,
not to pray.*

*Imagine
the effect
if we prayed
together.*

Table of Contents

Prologue 1

1 **Adoration** 5
   Father 5
   Son 8
   Spirit 11
   Word 14
   Love 16
   Creation 19
   Creativity 21
   Intimacy 24
   Worship 26
   Prayer 29
   Eternity 31
   Divinity 34
   Glory 36
   Sovereignty 39
   Locality 42

2 **Confession** 45
   Doubt 45
   Motives 48
   Greed 51
   Fear 54
   Sloth 56
   Ingratitude 59
   Pride 62
   Impatience 64
   Anger 67
   Judgment 70
   Secrecy 72
   Deceit 75
   Carnality 77
   Superiority 80

	Idolatry	83
3	**Thanksgiving**	86
	Relationship	86
	Blessing	89
	Family	91
	Discipline	94
	Trials	96
	Service	99
	Beauty	102
	Vocation	104
	Life	107
	Fellowship	109
	Redemption	112
	Resurrection	115
	Truth	117
	Rest	120
4	**Supplication**	123
	Provision	124
	Shelter	126
	Protection	129
	Communication	131
	Justice	134
	Healing	136
	Heart	139
	Families	141
	Generations	144
	Leaders	147
	Workers	149
	Teachers	152
	Students	155
	Lost	157
Epilogue		161
Index of Prayers		162

Prologue

"Pray to your Father, who is unseen." Matthew 6:6.

Father, hear our prayers. We pray because we want you close, familiar, even familial. We pray because we wish to be your brothers and sisters, sons and daughters, not foreign but family. While we read your word to know *of* you, we pray to *know you*. Through prayer, we seek intimacy with you that we share with no other, indeed that we cannot share with any other than you. Knowing *of* you makes us desire to *know you* not just like one knows a best friend but as a child knows one's own father or mother. We pray to you as the one who reared us. We pray as if we knew your every minute mannerism, indeed as all that ever mattered. While we see evidence of you in the magnificence and order of your creation, and see your action in events that others call chance or fortuity, we want more than representations, signs, and signals of you. Rather, we want you in the way that the tired crave rest, the hungry food, the thirsty drink, and the prisoner freedom. We pray longing for you in that deepest way that everything depends on it, as everything surely does so depend. This longing, this dependence is so because you created us in your image. You created us to look to you as a child looks to its father, and not any father, but to you who have all that any father should ever have and infinitely more so.

"How right they are to adore you!" Song of Songs 1:4.

Thus we pray always in adoration of you who are our Creator. We pray adoring you not perforce but because you are so deeply and mysteriously attractive, even enthralling and alluring to us. We need allure in our lives like we need breath. Life must have appeal, interest, and absorption because of the rich senses and fertile minds with which you blessed us. You gave us these gifts that we must use or we are not fully human. Life without allure would not be living but instead death waiting to happen. And so you have given us this critical need of not just imagining but of actively pursuing and worshiping you. You made us to need your actual embrace and to see the splendor and glory that you alone embody for us. Without your magnificence, without your boundless supply of grandeur, we fulfill that allure with weak and false things. Without you, we pursue intoxicants real and imagined that only distract, deplete, and destroy. You made us not for those things but for you to whom we pray in perfect pursuit. Hear our prayers of adoration.

"If we confess our sins, then he will forgive and purify us." 1 John 1:9.

We also pray in confession of our complete need for you. We have this need not only because you made us for you but also because you made us lost without you. We are so broken. The best of us are little more than facades stumbling our way through twists and turns made by our own helpless action and inaction. Without you, we are standardless. Without you, we judge our way by nothing other than self-interest, which is not judging at all but instead simply rationalizing ends that we pursue to satisfy our own sensations. Without you, we lose the grace and pace of your sensibility. We substitute our own sensuality for your sensibility, in ways that make us hurried, crude, and grasping. Without you, we are desperately finite, facing a certain demise that mocks our every paltry achievement and momentary pleasure. You alone have the power and will to lift us out of the prisons of our decay and corruption, and into your eternal light. Everything means nothing until we have you. With you, anything means everything. Even if they are far too seldom, Father, hear our prayers of confession.

"With thanksgiving, present your requests to God." Philippians 4:6.

We also pray in thanks, Father, so deeply appreciative of all who you are and all of what you do. We pray knowing our natural end and supernatural need for you. We take no stance toward you other than gratefulness, our gratitude gushing forth for your every frequent movement on our behalf. Meritless and helpless, we can claim no entitlement from you. As your creation, we lay prone on your sacred ground wholly at your mercy, thankful for first and last breath. Every gain in between we owe to your grace. We owe to you this rich life, sure order, and fabulous favor that you so surprisingly and generously bestow on us. We see the blessings that flow from you and accept them exactly as such. They are all yours to give as much as to withhold or even to take away. We accept gladly just what you deign to release. We begrudge nothing that you choose to refuse because all is yours and none ours unless you grant it to us. We take nothing from you that you do not choose to grant us. We only pray much and ask much, just as you would have us do. Father, hear our prayers of thanksgiving.

"Hear the supplications of your servant." 2 Chronicles 6:21.

We pray most often to you, though, Father, when our most-critical needs prompt us to do so. We pray in repeated supplication, purposeful petition, passionate plea, and simple request. Yes, we richly adore you, generously confess to you, and deeply thank you. Yet more often, we think of you and turn to you when we have such pressing needs. We pray asking of you, more than we pray venerating, esteeming, or revering you. Still, we do those other things, venerate, revere, and worship, too, whenever we think of and communicate with you, even in humble request. You know that we ask repeatedly, Father. Maybe you don't hold the frequency of our pleas against us but instead intend our needs to seem so constantly pressing. You then show yourself so attuned, attentive, and generous, as the best of fathers would do so and be so. We are your children, Father. You certainly know and may even intend that your children have many needs that only you can supply. Do not hold our pleas against us, even when you have already anticipated those needs and arranged and acted to meet them, as you constantly do. Our needs are so many that we could not possibly pray for all of our needs, even though we would do well with you to do so. Instead, accept our pleas not solely as motivating force but also as evidence that we know that we rely on you. Father, hear our prayers of supplication.

"Always pray, and do not give up." Luke 18:1.

Yet no matter the motivation or form of our prayers, Father, help us to pray often to you, like breathing. Let our every prayer draw us nearer to you until nothing separates us other than our resurrection-expectant flesh. Until that glorious resurrection, we have only prayer. We turn our thoughts to you, deep in our minds forming words that we intend to draw your attention to us even as we draw near you. We want you to look on us, to acknowledge that we who are your creation have turned to you so that you would show us that you see that we exist. We pray that you would participate with us. We pray that you would show us that we are not simply another brute thing that you made but instead deliberate and conscious beings who have willfully turned our attention to regard your splendor. You hear and know the words of our prayers. You know our prayers whether those prayers remain prisoners of our minds or break free in uttered breath. Our prayers wing straight to you even as they dissolve silently in our minds or we hear them dissipate into the wind. Extraordinarily, you listen. More extraordinarily, you then react and participate. Indeed, you answer and govern according not to our unholy condition but our righteous wish. How should we be so much to you, that you would answer prayer, other than that you made us in order that you would have human cause to answer? Hear these prayers, our Father, who are in heaven, as we hallow your name. And Father, respond.

1
Adoration

"How right they are to adore you!" Song of Songs 1:4.

Father, we do indeed adore you for all the reasons that the following prayers acknowledge. Beyond those reasons, we adore you simply for who you are, the one eternal creator God, and what you thus so rightfully command. How could we possibly adore any more so than you when we have none greater than you? None even approach anything akin to your wondrous glory. Indeed, our adoration of you comes not from us, not from our feeble intentions, but instead from you. The power and purpose of your presence evoke in us the only appropriate response, which is our unqualified, unreserved worship. If left to our own, then we might do no more than adore ourselves in fatal distraction. Instead, you show us that you are so much greater than anything that any of us could possibly be or even imagine. Thankfully, your magnificence leaves us no one to worship other than you. And so we do worship you. We think of you each hour, praying to you and about you each day. We constantly adore you, worshiping you as the only one so worthy. Father, hear our prayers of adoration.

Father

"Then God said, 'Let us make mankind in our image.'" Genesis 1:26.

PRAYER

You, Father, are the one to whom we look as children, nearly as very small children would look to their father. You tower over us as any father stands high over his smallest child. You possess stature, experience, knowledge, and powers that we your children can scarcely imagine. As is true with fathers in the eyes of their small children, you as our one great Father provide for us generously, richly, and completely without our even asking. You do so in mysterious ways. Your ways are so obscure to us as to seem both magical and effortless, except that we have other compelling evidence of your grace's great cost. You stand high above us not as a scolding, forbidding, or oppressive presence. You instead love us each individually with furious passion and depth. You seem to want to scoop each one of us up into your arms, just as a father would look down on his little children. When we come to you, we see you on your throne, exquisite, and yet even in your splendor you are somehow neither distant nor aloof. You instead invite our approach, wanting us to be near you, wanting to hear us. You made us for these very requests that we should ask of you, even while we celebrate your goodness, power, and generosity. How can we do anything other than adore you? We lift up our hands to you as a child lifts up hands when wanting a father to pick up the child. Lift us into your strong and gentle arms where we might receive your caresses of love, tenderness, and security. We having nothing beyond you, Father, neither need nor want, and we give you all.

Answer

I have indeed made you children in my very image and the image of my own Son, as any father must make none but children in his image. Your prayer I acknowledge because you speak truly of me, although little do you know of me. So very few truths are you yet able to speak. You have infinitely more wonders to discover of me, marvels that I cannot yet reveal to you until you are able both to comprehend and bear them. You know what little you need to know of me, even though I welcome and will fulfill your desire to learn more. You know for instance that you are indeed mine. I chose you for the good news that you carry of my Son. I have hidden you in my Spirit against the overwhelming glory of my wild love. My throne, of which you read in my word, you have not yet seen. Yet you will see my throne by persisting in the redemption and resurrection revealed in my Son. You, children, properly lift your hands to me, for you know that I have stretched out my Son's hands for you. My embrace of you, dear children, is now ready for you just as it is at all times. My embrace of you is perfect in its comfort, even though your heart may still have to prepare further in order to receive it. You glorify me appropriately, my children, for I am everything good that you will ever know. And so because you have adored me as your Father without asking anything in return, I will bless you as any good father would bless his children. I will bless you far more richly than the best father, in order that you may know that I answered your prayer of adoration.

TRANSFORMATION

He hadn't thought yet of just why providence had so richly blessed him as a father. He had no sense that he had earned or deserved the love and respect of so beautiful of a daughter. He didn't even remember praying that God would bless his wife and him with a devoted, God-loving daughter. Once she was born, though, both he and his wife had prayed earnestly and often that their daughter would know and follow the same Lord who had also rescued and so richly blessed them. He had no question that God moved in and through his daughter, and not only when his daughter showed her parents continual grace and kindness. She shared such kindness with everybody and did so in ministries serving others. His daughter so obviously carried the good Lord's servant heart, a heart indeed for other children. Just as he was reflecting on how or why he had come into such great fortune to have such a blessed child, he remembered how he had prayed in adoration of his divine Father. He had not asked the Father for a devoted child of his own but instead just revered God as Father. Yet just maybe, he thought for a moment, his prayer adoring his Father had stirred the Father's grace to bless him as a father. God could answer prayers even when they were only prayers of adoration, not prayers that made any particular request of him. Indeed, God might answer prayers of simple, unadorned adoration more often and richly than prayers making or adding requests. God knows what we need and desire even before we ask him. So why not pray primarily in adoration? Whether or not that was so, that God answered even prayers alone of adoration, he knew that he had the Father to thank for the blessing of a devoted child. He was so glad both that he had a divine Father to adore and that his own child adored the same Father while showing such grace to her earthly father.

REVELATION

He of course knew at his first glimpse that he was seeing the Father. The living being whose presence flooded everything around him was clearly in human form. Yet the Father was simultaneously so far beyond human, something so completely different, that he could only think of the Father as fully divine, indeed as the one God. He thought very briefly of taking stock of what he actually saw so that he could repeat it later to anyone to whom he described the moment. But he found himself utterly unable to catalog the encounter mentally, to register or log in his mind what he would somehow need to describe. For instance, the moment that he thought he might describe the Father's legs and arms as something strangely akin to glowing metal, the impression vanished into insignificance because the Father's legs and arms had already left other more-fantastic impression on him. He simply could not describe what he saw because his mind was unable to comprehend God adequately. He realized shortly later that other beings or illusions might take on fantastic forms, so that whatever he saw at the time might be deceiving him in making him think that he was seeing God. But his heart, mind, and soul all immediately and utterly convinced him that he was in the Father's presence. No being other than God, and certainly no illusion, could possibly so fill his every fiber, not merely with emotion but with an exquisite fullness that left no room at all. When one meets one's Creator, one has nothing left unfilled. That moment when he realized that he was losing the last bit of himself in full embrace of the Father's glory, was when another image distracted his attention, thankfully. He sensed that his continued contemplation of the Father's glory might at any moment end somehow in his annihilation, not that he would or could have in the least resisted it.

Son

"Anyone who has seen me has seen the Father." John 14:19.

PRAYER

Father, we rejoice in having your glorious Son as your incarnate image. We adore how in your Son you gave us the perfect picture of who you are. With the image of your Son, we can now more readily worship who you are, what you think, and what you do. We also know so much more clearly what you expect of us. You need not have revealed yourself so clearly and completely as you did in your Son, but you chose out of love to do so. You revealed yourself in your Son's form not simply to show your powerful allure and demonstrate your miracle-working service. You also revealed your Son for his sacrificial mission, which was to give us, so far from your holiness, a path back to you. What can we say of your Son other than that we adore him and through him adore you even more? In the record of the Gospels, we hang on his every word. We study his every movement and weep at his every sacrificial service on our behalf, knowing that you, oh God, would stoop so low as to walk among your broken and needful people. What gift you have given us in your Son. What glory we see in you through your Son, the one whom we take as our sole guide and model, to whom we cling to carry us back to you. We worship you because the blood of your Son has freed us from every one of our besetting sins. He paid every penny that we owe to you, giving us footing before you as if we too were your children. So perfect of a Father as you could not accept anything less than perfect children, which is precisely how we stand before you, after you washed and cleansed us completely by having given your Son for us. We adore your Son, Father, just as we adore you.

ANSWER

You are right to adore my Son, for in his worship you also worship me. No one who rejects my Son can know me. My Son is my image and his sacrificial salvation the only way the unholy wash pure to regain me. Keep to my Son, you of frequent prayer. Indeed, pray in his name. I hear no prayer from your own unclean heart and lips, but prayer in his name reaches me. I am, I create, and I love in order to glorify my Son, just as my Son lives, serves, and loves to glorify me. As I breathed my Spirit into my Son, so my Son has breathed my Spirit into you that you may know my Son and through him know me. Every image that you have of my Son is an image that you know of me. His words are my words, and his will is my will. Take of him and eat, and drink of his blood, for his life is the life through which you will live eternally with me. Do not mix the blood of my Son, which is the sacrifice I made for you, with the blood of any other sacrifice, which is no sacrifice at all. Such efforts are only your vanity. Do what my Son tells you to do because my Son says only what he hears from me. Listen to my Son, love my Son, accept my Son, and know what my Son has done for you. He did for you precisely as his doing so pleased me. My painful pleasure was that my Son would bring you to me. In doing so, my Son brought my glory to him, my Son given for you glorified my Son for both him and for me. And so because you have adored my Son, I will strengthen your desire for him. I will reassure you that you draw as you trust from him, until you will have the full joy and confidence of your salvation.

Transformation

The two of them, husband and wife, shared a powerful love for Jesus. Neither of them could really pinpoint who or what was the inspiration for their great and ever-growing love for their Lord, or when or where that love had arisen. All that they knew was that his love and comfort continued to grow in them, just as they desired to draw closer to him. He already surrounded them, his love for them already burning brightly within them. They wept more often in joy with him and more often felt his glory suffuse them. They saw more of his magnificent work in large and small things and sensed his powerful presence more often in others who pursued him like them. Neither of them felt any more righteous or holy, if anything seeing instead their natural selves as ever more debased. Still, they shared the sense that Jesus was carrying them powerfully upward with him, in ever greater joy and confidence, along their earthly journey. Then one day, in a quiet moment together, both of them considered the possibility that their prayers of adoration for the Son had somehow stimulated in their Father his desire that they would indeed know the Son's full glory. Whether or not their prayers revering the Son had informed the Father, they were daily more sure that in due time they would indeed know and celebrate the Son's great glory.

Revelation

He supposed that he could have described the first startling form in which he saw the Son as that of a slain lamb. He knew that image from scripture, as most others followers also know it, and so the image did instantly occur to him. Yet the Son seemed simultaneously to be not just in the form of a lamb but also in human form, although marred nearly beyond human likeness. No matter, though, what specific form the startling image actually took, he was clearly seeing the slain Son. The form unmistakably conveyed that the Son had given his life on the cruel cross after horrific scourging and further torture. Yet somehow, despite the Son's marred image, nothing about the Son was inglorious. Indeed, to the contrary, the Son's disfigurement, although breathtaking in its brutality, seemed at once to elevate rather than diminish the Son's inherent glory. The Son, though, was not simply a static form as he comprehended it. The disfigured but fully glorified man-or-lamb Son instead approached the seated Father from whom the Son's movement had distracted his attention. He knew the scripture about the slain lamb taking the scroll from the right hand of the seated One. Here, though,

Son and Father did not exchange a scroll but something more like an embrace. Or perhaps they had always been simply One, divided only for a few moments for him to see briefly their complementary images. While he was using his eyes and mind to comprehend the glorious embrace, he also clearly sensed that he was understanding only a small part of what he saw. All that he could be sure was that he had first seen Father, and now he had seen Son.

Spirit

"True worshippers will worship the Father in the Spirit." John 4:23.

PRAYER

We also rejoice, Father, in your Holy Spirit, the comforter and counselor whom you sent us after so gloriously sharing your Son with us. We adore your Spirit. We adore the one whom you sent to call so gently and persistently to our minds your words and that wondrous life and image of your Son. We would be lost without your Spirit, aggrieved and adrift at the loss of your Son. But your Spirit instead settles on us at times like a dove, bringing us comfort and confidence. Your Spirit settles on us at other times like a flame, giving us the passion and purpose to share testimony of your Son. We treasure every movement of your Spirit. We embrace every reminder that your Spirit brings us of your Son's work in carrying out your will and purpose. We listen carefully for your Spirit's whispered voice. We discern sensitively for your Spirit's subtle allure. We watch closely for the faint images of your Son that your Spirit shows us. We do all of these things so that we can draw closer to you, rely more heavily on you, and pursue your will in all that we think and do. Show us more of your Spirit, Father. Keep our spirits still that we may see your Spirit's movement. Keep our mouths quiet that we may hear more of your Spirit's voice. And keep our minds clear that your Spirit may fill us with thoughts of you and your Son. Then give us your Spirit's passion to do as you will. Make us followers of your Spirit, moved consistently and purposefully by your Spirit's discerning guide. Father, we adore your Holy Spirit in whom we rejoice.

ANSWER

So, too, are you right to adore my Spirit, just as you adore me and adore my Son. You should indeed embrace my Spirit because my Spirit is the one of us who is now with you. I gave you my Spirit as your guide and comforter when I lifted the ancient gates for my resurrected Son as the first of many more through him to come. I did not want you left alone when my Son returned to me. I wanted you to have my Spirit with you so that you could also have the words, life, and presence of my Son even while anticipating your own resurrection. And so yes, venerate my precious Spirit. Hear my Spirit, living in and through my Spirit even as my Spirit lives in you. Do not fight or offend my Spirit. My Spirit moves swiftly like a wind in the treetops, gently like an alighting dove, and powerfully like a descending flame. When you sense my Spirit, let my Spirit enter you that you may know my will and do the work for which my Spirit comes, which is the will and work glorifying both me and my Son. Let my Spirit vitalize and animate you for that wonder for which I made you, which is to enter my kingdom in worship and fellowship with my Son. And because you have adored and welcomed my Spirit, I will send you an unmistakable remembrance that my Spirit is around you and with you and in you, blessing you with ever deeper relationship with my Son and me. You will afterward sense my Spirit's presence and feel my holy breath in every rustling wind.

TRANSFORMATION

He had never experienced anything like it and was pretty sure that he never again would. The event hadn't lasted much longer than a moment and was so bizarre that afterward he thought for a time that he'd just chalk it up to pure imagination and forget it. Yet at the same time he knew that he would never forget it. He hadn't imagined it, either, but instead had experienced something so unlikely and unprecedented as to attribute it squarely and fairly to the divine. The sensation had come at the perfect moment and in the perfect setting, exactly when and where it should. He had been calm, unexcited, but attuned. Then it happened. Something like a circle of energy, a buzzing enlightening band of living electricity had alighted on the very crown of his head and then slowly descended from his head to his toes. The presence was so palpable that he had looked around first to see if he was literally electrified and then to see if others around him were electrified, too. Nothing was out of the normal. He appeared to be the only one experiencing anything unusual. The descending band suffused him with something like an open energy and revealing light. Had he not been so in control of his circumstances and indeed actively engaged with the others around him, he would have succumbed to emotion, riven by the band's pure energy and light. But the band did not demand that submission or anything else of him. It had just alighted, descended through him, and then gone, leaving him changed forever. And though he disliked speculation and tended strongly to the rational, he nonetheless felt that he knew what, or rather Who, it was.

Revelation

In the embrace or union of Father and approaching Son, he saw something else that he could not describe but that somehow still immediately conveyed to him its profound meaning. As Father and Son met and conjoined, something akin to an aura, force, or field issued or emanated from their union. Yet although aura-like in appearance, the emanating field was not simply a force. Rather, the emanation was a living being whom he instantly recognized as the Holy Spirit. He had of course read the scriptures portraying the Spirit's descent first as a dove and later as flames. What or whom he saw could, he later supposed, have been either bird-like or flame-like. The Spirit's appearance was that inexplicable. He couldn't exactly say how he knew that the Spirit lived as a being, except that the Spirit just so obviously observed the Father and Son, and even observed and regarded him, consciously, knowingly, like the way in which people instantly distinguish persons from robots or cartoons. The Spirit lived as the Spirit's own entity, even though the Spirit issued from and was entirely of the unity of Father and Son. The Spirit was also every bit as engrossing and wondrous in appearance as had been the Father and Son. Indeed, to say that he had looked upon any or all of them from some distance away, aloofly, as an uninvolved observer, would be inaccurate. The Spirit was at once some distance away, emanating into trinity from the unity of the Father and Son, while also all around him. He could no more have moved away from the Spirit than to have moved into or toward the Spirit because the Spirit was all around him and even in him. Indeed, the Spirit seemed to accomplish the same effect with respect to the Father and Son. The moment that the Spirit had emanated from the unity of Father and Son, the Spirit had also brought the presence of the Father and Son to him, into him, and all around him. He could not have advanced toward or retreated from any of them, Father, Son, or Spirit, had he in any way wished, which he didn't wish. He at that moment did not need breath, circulation, or any other vital sign of life, for the author of life was in and all around him, utterly suffusing and vitalizing him. The Spirit had won him.

Word

"The Word was God." John 1:1.

PRAYER

Father, we celebrate and adore your word, indeed your Word made flesh as your Son. You spoke, and what you spoke was so. When you who are the author of life speak a living word into dead bones, they rise adorned anew with flesh and life. Because your word is living, your word acts on things. Your word changes conditions, transforms situations, and divides spirit from soul, discerning the attitudes of the mind and condition of the heart. As we read your word, we do not judge your word, but your word judges us, guiding us into your holiness and righteousness. Without your word, we would be lost souls, hopeless souls, souls without present faith or future life. For these reasons, we cherish your word, embrace your word, read your word in awe and joy. We adore you for your word, without which we would not have you. We know you through your word. Indeed, your own word says that your word is you, flesh made word, word made flesh, to communicate and commune with us. Glory to your word, honor to your word, praise to your word, unchanging, spoken once, written once, living once, and lasting from here to forever. Give us more of your word, Father, bring us to your word, reveal yourself to us through your word. We need nothing and no one more than we need your holy Word.

ANSWER

You are also right to adore my Word, you who in my Spirit pray to me in the name of my beloved Son. You would first not be here had my Word not brought you forth. Then without my Word, you would not know me. My Word brought you to life as we spoke of creation and creation came to be. My Word then brought you back to life, calling and redeeming you to eternal life, after you gave up life in vain attempt to be the equal of me. So indeed heed and glorify my Word, oh children of mine, as my Word glorifies, seeks, and speaks of me. When I send my Word forth, my Word brings back to me that for which I sent my Word. You are for whom I sent my Word forth, you and others who confess your depravity and turn from your debaucheries that my Son's sacrifice may lift you to me. You have listened to my Word, accepted and embraced my Word. As long as you do so, as long as you listen to my Spirit to continue to hew to my Son, then you have not only my Son and Spirit but also have me. You will see my glory, and in seeing my glory, you will know why I first created you and then brought you back to life in order that you may share in the worship of the one who made you to worship only me. Follow my Word, you who pray in adoration of me. My Word leads you to me, where you will have all you have ever desired by giving all that you have to me. And because you adore my Word, I will make my Word not a cold text on screen or printed page but living and active within you.

TRANSFORMATION

She realized one day that she no longer knew God's word merely as a set of rules, stories, or principles. She couldn't identify any particular moment that the words of the Bible had gone from sound instruction to nearly like something or someone living within her. As she turned the thought over in her mind, she decided that the sense of an active and dynamic presence within her was exactly what she felt when she meditated on God's word. She had long revered the Bible, had long treated it as the divine word and story of God. But its words, phrases, verses, passages, and even whole books were no longer only a record, even if a magnificent record, of Father and Son. No, the Bible's words were now more to her, particularly those words that Jesus had uttered or that described Jesus and the meaning of things that Jesus had said, accomplished, and represented. Those words had a way of changing her mind about things and, more than her mind, changing her heart about persons and situations. The effect wasn't merely that the words convinced her to take different paths, think different thoughts, speak different statements, and perform different services, all with different attitude, more patiently, persistently, and joyfully. The words' effect was less like argument and more like mentoring and modeling. She was doing the will of another, of the Father and Son, as if they were doing it ahead of her and with her, as if they had planned things for her. As she finished these thoughts of the powerful living effect of God's Word, she committed to pray even more often in the Word's adoration.

REVELATION

Her first impression of Jesus as the word of God was anything but what she expected. In retrospect, though, the startling event made perfect sense. It was thus like everything else that came directly from God. The event was entirely apart from mere human design and intention, and thus holy. She had been meditating on Jesus, as she often did, simply adoring him deep in her heart, bringing herself to near the point of tears, as often happened. Yet just in that moment that her heart seemed to melt into his exquisite presence, a great sword emerged painlessly from deep within her. The sword, fully the size of a man, shimmered gloriously for a moment before her, as if to show her how sharp its double edges were. She even recalled looking down to see if the sword had riven her in two in its awesome emergence. Perhaps she was right then dying. Just as she began to wonder at the incredible emergence of this spectacular sword, and indeed just as she began to fear the peril in which she now stood, the sword was no longer a sword but a man whom she instantly recognized as her Lord Jesus Christ. In that instant recognition, she lost all fear and instead began to melt again as she had been doing just when the sword had emerged. He smiled broadly and gently at her as no person had ever managed before. He then tossed his head back and laughed a joyous laugh, not at all at her but instead with the unspoken invitation that she join in his laughter, which to her surprise she found herself doing. As if satisfied at her reassurance that he had meant no harm but only revelation, he then disappeared, leaving her still laughing and weeping for joy, all at once. She had long known the scriptures that described the word of God coming from Christ's mouth like a sword. His word, so sharp as to be living and active, had indeed given her a new heart. And he had now made for her a joyous celebration of the formerly frightening sword image.

Love

"God is love." 1 John 4:16.

PRAYER

Father, we celebrate and adore your love. We adore that you are who you are, having given us that you are love. We also treasure that you created us in order that you might care for us. You created us not just to care for us but to love us so deeply as to give for us your only Son. We celebrate that you made your love the heart of your created universe when you could instead have turned your back to your creation and to us. Your Son demonstrated your love for us. He accepted your will that he would die for us in order that we might live again for you and with you. Your Son restored us to you whom we lost so long ago and so surely in our depravity. You would care for us only because you love and are love. Your love is unique, a wondrous giving yourself up for us through which you order, vitalize, and justify your creation. We love you because you first loved us. You were patient and kind with us. You did not fall easily into anger against us. You kept no record of our wrongs, instead protecting us and then when we turned from you nonetheless persevering with us. Your love never fails us. When everything else disappears, your love will not disappear but will instead reveal everything about us and show us everything that we do not yet know of you. Even though we do not see you, we hold onto faith in you, first hoping and trusting that you will do as you have said for us and then finally knowing that you will do so because you are love and cannot deny yourself. Father, we adore you because you are love.

ANSWER

You rightly venerate my love for you and my creation, for I am love. No love exists other than that love that comes from me. I so loved those of you to whom I gave life in the world that I gave my Son for you, wanting you to accept the good-news mission on which I sent him in order that you would have eternal life with me. Love is nothing more nor less than my having sent my beloved Son to you that he would do as I wished by giving his life for your life. You speak of love as many things, but love has no true meaning other than this life-giving mission that my Son and I shared with you. Because I am love, you have no other love than this most-loving thing that I could do for you. Because I loved my Son, I reserved for him to do that which would glorify him beyond any other possible thing. I wanted my Son to have my glory, to be love as I am love. He received my glory when he gave his life as my plan was for him, to bring you to me through him. You do not know love unless you know my Son and know my plan and purpose for my Son, that purpose which he so gloriously fulfilled. If you know my Son, then you know love, and you, too, can live in love as my Son lives in my love and I live in him. When you adore my love, you adore me, because I am love, and all love is from me. And so because you have adored my love, just as I desired that you do, I will send friend and enemy to test and refine you to hold my Spirit that you may both know and show my love, as I must do for all whom I love.

Transformation

For the first time, in the middle of another meditation on God's great love, he felt that he might have long misunderstood and mistaken love for something less than what God actually meant by it. With all of the challenges that he had faced just trying to live a decent life, challenges as often coming from friends as from enemies, he had thought that he was missing something in God's love, as if he hadn't gotten his God-relationship right. The Father had loved his Son with what was surely the most perfect and intense love. Yet the Father had also given his Son what was just as surely the hardest of all missions. Maybe God's love wasn't sentimental, soft, and sweet, he realized. Maybe God's love was not at all as if it would lead to a life of perfect ease. Maybe God instead demonstrated his love in ways that shaped the recipient into someone whom God could love even more. Love's purpose was not ease, sweetness, laughter, and light but instead closer relationship. He did find that the challenges that God had allowed him to face were just the things to change him. They tested how much he would rely on God while increasing the necessity of his relying. He had no question that he was different, that he loved God more because of hard challenges. He could not really attribute that difference to the blessings that God had shared as much as to the challenges that God had allowed. Maybe God was showing his love for him not just or primarily in daily joyful ease but instead in the defining challenges.

Revelation

The next aspect of his encounter with the unified Father and Son, and emanating Spirit, was something that his imagination had long anticipated. The emanating Spirit somehow turned his attention away from the Father, Son, or Spirit as objects. The Spirit turned his attention instead to the filling that he had felt with each observation in turn first of Father, then Son, and finally Spirit. That suffused sense was not simply emotion. It certainly evoked emotion, indeed exquisite emotion that might have devolved into ecstasy had the Spirit not somehow cautioned him silently against it. He understood instantly that the suffusion was not for his pleasure. Rather, he gathered in a sort of meeting of the minds, Spirit to human observer, that the suffusion was love. He sensed both the filling of God who is love *and* that God loved him. Either one of those fillings in purest form would naturally have produced ecstasy, although again, the Spirit had restrained him from it. He now clearly understood that the Spirit in emanation from Father and

Son was carrying their will to him. He then turned his attention for the first time to others who were also present. He hadn't really noticed these others, who much like him were simply regarding the Godhead, until the Spirit had caused him to do so. As he observed these others, he felt the suffusion of God's love going out to each of them. This outward-flowing love was so different from God's inward-flowing love but simultaneously so alike it. The outward flow occurred much in the manner that he had for all of his former life wished it. He had just never quite been able to share such life, except perhaps for his own wife and child at too-rare times. He had been unable to send out that immense suffusion as he was now effortlessly doing. The others to whom he effortlessly directed this immense suffusion of God's love knew it, he realized by their silent acknowledgment, making the event even more profoundly wondrous.

Creation

"Creation waits eagerly for God's children." Romans 8:19.

PRAYER

Even as we eagerly embrace and celebrate your Son and Holy Spirit, Father, so splendidly revealing you, we also perceive you through your creation, for which we further adore you. You gave us a paradise that we lost. You then mercifully banished us only to our present home, paradise's near neighbor. Even more mercifully, you beckon us back to our future paradise home. Your beacon flaming sword flashes back and forth at paradise's entrance, both guarding and inviting us to your tree of life, your Son lifted up for us. Our present near-paradise home confirms your proximity, confirms how close we are to you. Only the degree to which we foolishly resist your Son separates us from you. We lose you only when we turn our backs on your Spirit's persistent entreaties. Oh, Father, let your creation turn us again to you and your Son. Help us to see your mercy in the daily dawn, your care in the plentiful harvest, and your power in the gathering storm. Remind us to feel your vitality in the brisk morning, your comfort in the warming sun, and your caress in the afternoon's light breeze. We see splendor, order, growth, conservation, regeneration, and your other magnificent workings all around us, each of them drawing us closer to you. Father, we adore you through the bounty, beauty, and care of your creation. You are our merciful and generous Father.

ANSWER

You rightly speak to me of the glory of my creation, of which you are not just any part but instead my special design, made in my image. Even though I am your creator and you the created, I have given you knowledge of me, your creator. That knowledge that you have of me, even though you are my own creation, should be your constant wonder, for what thing can know of he who made it? The difference between you and any other created thing is that I gave *my* life to you, breathing into you my Spirit. I did not merely create you but also shared my life with you, bringing you into family and fellowship with me. When you had given up that fellowship, I then sent you my Son in whom is the fullness of my life. I sent my Son in order that you may return to me after learning more of me through my Son. You are my creation, and I am your creator, just as I created all. Never think of me as created or as merely part of my creation. I am instead the never-created one who existed before I brought forth time and creation. You can never know all of me because I hold all worlds in me. As my creation, you are of this world, while I am not of this world even when I am in this world. My Son was in the world, and now he is with me. My Spirit is in my creation, just as you are in my creation. Know my Spirit who shows me to you and shows you my Son. In my Spirit, you transcend your created condition to know of and dwell in me. And so because you have revered me through my creation, I will show you more of the magnificence of my creation. You will see splendor after splendor, each time turning to me in worship.

TRANSFORMATION

She found that she was beginning to have to shield her eyes, to look away from the many magnificent creations that God was showing her. She couldn't trace her growing sensation of wonder to any particular vision or moment. She just felt increasingly over-awed, a feeling that she sensed ever more frequently when seeing for the first time yet another one of God's sublimely superb designs. The sensation seemed to just creep up on her, budding and growing within her until she wanted to weep at what she saw. Those moments sometimes foreshadowed themselves in things like a tree's blossoming wonder on a gorgeous spring day or the emerging beauty of a spectacular sunset. But the events also often took her by complete surprise, as when she encountered a tiny new flower embedded in wild dune grass or glimpsed the stunningly high flight of a distantly trumpeting swan. Towering storm clouds building in the late afternoon, shafts of light angling through red-orange skies, perfectly glassy seas in a nothing-but-gray dawn, and spider webs in the tall grass holding jewels of dew all arrested her attention. One after another, these surprising new perspectives showed her God's exquisite designs. She also looked at the tiny hand of her infant child, imagining what wonders God would work through that irresistible bundle of joy.

REVELATION

God's kingdom, in which she now dwelled solely and continuously, was indeed a divine creation. Her earthly home had shown her many of God's wonders, so much that she would occasionally have to turn away from them for their overwhelming splendor. Yet there, the world's corruption, indeed her own corruption and limitations, mediated the wonder of God's creation. Creation there only intimated the creator. By contrast, in God's kingdom everything that she countenanced reflected God's glory in unmediated fashion. His presence lit the sky, nourished the fruits, and cooled the waters. Thus, everything that she saw or touched completely healed and utterly satisfied her. No tears fell in God's kingdom because every created thing reflected the full presence of God. God was not animate within his created things, even in his own kingdom, but God was present unmediated by any corruption of creation. Everywhere she turned, she knew that God was fully present, because everywhere she turned, sin was absent, all was perfect, and nothing corrupted. To say that the kingdom was spectacular was almost unnecessary or even incorrect. The kingdom's features bore remarkable resemblance to her former earthly abode except for the complete absence of any distortion. That purity, holiness, and divinity was what made the kingdom so healing, so satisfying, and so wondrous. She felt like her kingdom explorations were exactly as they should have been on earth but never were on earth. They were endlessly exciting, always nurturing, always adventurous, and always successful because they always encountered and honored God. She now understood the purpose and nature of God's spectacular creation.

Creativity

"He created all things through him and for him." Colossians 1:16.

PRAYER

We also adore you, Father, for creativity, not only for your creation and your willingness to create but for the creative capacities with which you bless us. You first brought forth creation and yet still continue to make new things and old things new. Indeed, you form each one of us uniquely to reflect your infinite array of magnificent attributes. You then create spectacular vistas, events, and visions in which we see you, even while forming us to create our own settings, scenes, scores, and displays that direct our attention toward you, representing and venerating you. You imbue us with this urge to create because you are the creator, we are your image, and you made us to worship you creatively. You allow us to revel in your creativity, to marvel at the wondrous things that you bring forth, even as your agents we share in their creation. You employ us like paintbrushes to color your canvas each day anew, weaving myriad events into good circumstances, relationships, and works that you planned and created for us to do. You give us the will, methods, and means to create, but more so, you give us the purpose to create, which is solely to worship and adore you. Father, we embrace your creativity even as we embrace our own creativity with which you infuse us for you.

ANSWER

You should indeed revere that I create wonders such as you and that I extend my creativity to you and through you. I made you and made all that with which you create, while I also gave you my desire to create. You are creative because I, the supreme creator, created you in my image with my desire to create. So yes, fulfill my creative desire, revel in my creative capacity, but create only as doing so honors me and as I authorize and plan for you. Turn away from pride in your creations, for you create only as I imbue you. You create nothing that rivals me, because all you create lies within that which I made of you and for you. In your creations, acknowledge and honor me. Your creations are temporary and bounded, like you, while my creations are infinite and eternal, as I am infinite and eternal. Only I, who am without bounds, generate that which is without bounds, and is infinite and eternal. So make things that reflect me, your creator, and my love for you, calling others to my kingdom in which all is glorious, new, and eternal. Show with that which you create the possibilities for you that I hold, the greatest of which is to follow my Son into my kingdom of the eternal. Create as I would have you create, honoring me and my Son, and create nothing other. And because you honor me as your creator and author of your creative capacity, I am giving you the will, passion, and means to create abundantly, which you will then do in my honor.

TRANSFORMATION

Even as he aged, and in his age more often grew weary, he sensed a growing desire to create. He hoped that neither pride nor ego drove his growing creative passion, as he sensed that they drove the creative passions of some others. He had no particular desire that others know him for what he did. Instead, he felt a growing responsibility, opportunity, and commitment to create as a way to reflect the goodness and creativity of God. Oh, he had no illusion that his modest creations, such as they were, had any real hope of representing God's creative majesty. In fact, he could not point to anything creative that he did, artistic, literary, or otherwise, that had any relative merit or distinction. He knew that his talents, again such as they were, were entirely common and ordinary, at best average among the talents of others, and thus his creations nothing in which to take pride, which wasn't his interest in any case. Rather, he wanted to exercise to his full capacity the very ordinariness with which God had so clearly marked him. He didn't want to be special in anyone's eyes other than the eyes of God, and not even there for the quality of his works but rather for the extent of his devotion. And oddly, he even took no credit for his will to create in God's honor, as perfectly though humbly as he could. Even his passion for productive action he attributed fully to a generous God.

REVELATION

His first kingdom encounter with God's creativity was a myth-exploding wonder. Marveling as always at the kingdom's perfect creation all around him, he had just begun to reflect on God's having at once created it, just as he had from scripture long imagined in his earthly days how God had first created the universe. Just at that moment that he began again to surmise God's long-ago creative burst, as he had so surmised in his earthly days, God revealed himself as engaged right then in the most extraordinary creative actions. He took his observation, he was then and later sure correctly so, to be God *still in the act* of creating. In the instant revelation, like other revelations so sudden and unexpected, God had meant, he was again sure, to correct his prior misimpression. God had not set the universe in mechanical action eons ago, like having built and then wound up a spring-driven clock or watch, to leave it alone as it wound down. That myth God's revelation to him had just exploded. God was constantly, but for a day's rest, making anew. God was knitting together multitudes of new lives in the womb. He was bringing forth new growth in the spring while over summer preparing new fall harvests. He was starting new churches and fostering new faith. God was constantly making all things new in endless, glorious, abundant creation. Just how God revealed himself as at once creating vast new was nearly impossible for him to describe. He supposed that God's form looked briefly like an intense star out of which new things exploded in all direction. Nearly as strangely, he could just feel at that moment of the form's spectacular appearance that his own creative urge somehow arose out of or through God's own super-abundant creativity. Apparently, he had in his earthly creativity never really been making new things of his own but only tentatively connecting with, and very likely grossly distorting, God's spectacular creative abundance of perfect new things.

Intimacy

"God's intimate friendship blessed my house." Job 29:4.

PRAYER

Your intimacy draws us to you, too, Father. Your allure holds us in thrall. Although you strike awe and even holy fear in us, you also made us for your affectionate relationship. You alone satisfy the closeness that we crave, that strong sense that we have of wanting to be creation's integral part. We want to engage and involve ourselves not just creatively and productively but as an insider, knowing and known, respecting and respected, loving and loved. You give us that intimacy like no other, satisfying our craving like nothing else satisfies. You dissolve our isolation, break down our corporeal walls, take us in, and hold us as your own. You stop time, stop words, and stop thought, substituting for them the proximity and immediacy that time, words, and thought all pursue. While relinquishing nothing of your sovereignty, authority, and power, you nonetheless offer us a tenderness beyond anything that we otherwise would know. You melt hearts, still the will, and bring floods of tears that are neither sadness nor joy but only life utterly fulfilled. You leave nothing wanting, nothing untouched, nothing unsatisfied, nothing unknown. Your intimacy quells all desire, Father. You answer every need, for which we adore you.

ANSWER

You are my intimate companion, mine whom I made for nearest fellowship, in whom my Son and Spirit also rejoice. You are precious to me, my own possession, whose attention I covet and over whom I am jealous when you turn instead to your idols, none of which are as great or worthy of your attention as me. I want you close, invite you close, that you may know and adore only me. My jealousy though is not that of a competitor but of your maker. I alone have righteous claim to your devotion because you would not exist, indeed you would cease to be, without me. And my intimacy is not your downfall but your salvation because your life would be only temporary without my proximity. Thus you have every just right and good reason to pursue my intimacy, through which you grow mature, vital, wise, and strong. My intimacy is good for you, best for you, making of you whom I intended when I gave life to you from the womb. If you want to be someone of distinction for anything of good or value, then you must first be someone close to me. For my intimacy, I made you. Draw close, oh you children of prayer, draw very, very close to me. Hear my breath, feel it upon you, as my Spirit gives you comfort, purpose, and life. And because you have recognized and submitted to my allure, I will fill you with the satisfaction of my intimacy. In me, you will find the relief and release that nothing else can supply you.

TRANSFORMATION

She had of course long heard of God's intimacy, of how his cherishing those who drew close to him would fill, comfort, and satisfy them. She had not, though, expected that his intimacy would be as satisfying as it had proven that it was. When praying that God would draw her close, she had imagined that his doing so would still her mind and tranquilize her emotions, ease her anxiety and bring her contentment at last. For some inexplicable reason, she hadn't imagined that his intimacy would include what it did, not just the serenity that she expected but also an exultation of mind, sense, and emotion. In retrospect, she felt that she had been wrong to think that God's intimacy would mean solace and stillness alone, something like a disturbed child finally coming to rest in its mother's comforting arms. Nearness to God, she later recognized, would of course have included much more than calming immobility. Utter trust in fulfilled dependency would indeed bring such calm, but mixing those settling assurances with fearsome love, passion, and awe, would of course also produce exulting joy. Until God blessed her so, and he managed to do so often, she hadn't thought possible the joining together of such exquisite exhilaration with such perfect peace. This intimacy, she then realized, must be like the kingdom's eternity. Even though she prayed for his intimacy often, she had little sense of why God would actually grant her such privilege, other than that she so completely embraced his beloved Son in whose name she made her frequent requests for intimacy.

REVELATION

She had in her earthly days given substantial thought to the intimacy that she hoped to enjoy in the kingdom. She had of course had moments of it even then, she hoped intimating much greater intimacy to come. What she hadn't realized then though was that intimacy would be no kingdom concern whatsoever. Previously, she had longed for intimacy and only rarely found it, and then only partially. Of course in the kingdom (and she was later surprised that she hadn't thought of it), she had no such longing. God was constantly present in the kingdom in unmediated, although certainly appropriately restrained, form. Because she had constant access to his love and goodness, she had no sense of waiting for intimacy to arise, within her soul to congeal into something that she could sense and grasp, on which to draw. She instead drew on God constantly. The surprising thing that she did not and should not have anticipated was that the form or mechanism through which God supplied his constant kingdom intimacy varied. It was not that Jesus suddenly appeared to her, and then she felt him close. Rather, she felt his sustaining and enlarging proximity in everything including the light, air, vistas, and vegetation. And she did not only feel in everything that he might soon approach. He was *there*, as if she could at any moment fall at his feet to hug and weep over them, whether she necessarily saw him or not. Every moment was a walk, talk, dance, song, adventure, meal, or other moment with Jesus. In retrospect, his constant kingdom intimacy made perfect sense. She just hadn't expected how instant, simple, perfect, boundless, and inexhaustible those moments would be.

Worship

"'Worshipers must worship in Spirit and truth.'" John 4:24.

PRAYER

Your intimacy, Father, is prelude to our worship of you. We are more than merely close to you. We more than merely draw from your nearness. We also reverence you, lifting our hearts, hands, and voices in your praise. Although you made us in your image, we are infinitely far from your equals. You are maker, and we are your made. Our closeness to you thus simply reminds us of how much greater you are than us. Even as we draw so near, you still count us, consider us, overtake us, and govern and rule us. If you did not so mercifully shield your enormity, vastness, and greatness from us, then you would obliterate us alone by your presence. We need so badly to worship you, you without whom we would die in worship of ourselves. In venerating you, we save ourselves, giving up the life that we cannot create or hold to you who creates us and gives us life. In you alone do we find that unoriginated incarnation, vastness, and significance that we know as eternity. You were before, and you will be after. You are outside of time, beyond place, preexistent and post-existent, life inherent, suffused, and imbued. Language cannot hold you for you are the incorporeal word, the author of all meaning, indeed of life itself. Words utterly fail, leaving us only to reverence you, Father, adoring that we have you to worship.

ANSWER

I accept all of your heartfelt worship. I object to your worship when it honors only your performances, but I bask in your authentic praise that you shower on me. I gladly, even joyfully, accept your common worship among fellow followers. I especially embrace your public praise, when you dance and bow before me in the presence of others who would prefer that you dance and bow before them. I also accept your quiet praises that others do not observe at all but that you direct in secret to me. You rightly worship me because you have none other than me. No one has done for you as I have done, and no one can do for you as I will do. Although you grasp little of all that I am, you know enough of me to worship me in holy fear. You know too that as you worship, I will show you more of me. You will see of me things that will cause you to fall prostrate in awe, even as I then strengthen you. Stand on your feet, and open your eyes to see more of me. Worship me deeply, my follower, for in my worship you will not only see wonders for which your tired eyes long, but you will also see why I made you as I did. You will see why I placed you where I did and what you are to do next for me. I assure you of these good things because you have worshipped me.

Transformation

Worship grew on him for seasons that stretched into years and then decades, not that how he felt about worship was what mattered. He had learned instead that worship was about what God received, not what he received, although at the same time he knew that God would bless him for every worship that he offered. Through those seasons that had stretched into years and then decades, he had the growing sense that time away from worship was desert time, dry time, nearly but not quite pointless time. He had in those dry times to convince himself that one worshipped God not just in gathered and celebratory throng but also in the quiet moments of contemplation and even in the busy moments of service. In a good life, all of life is worship. Every righteous act and word venerates the glorious one who gives life and the ability to enjoy, share, and reflect on it. He knew that he only scant imagined the reality, power, and picture of his worship's object. He understood that if God had shown him more of himself, then he would have abandoned for abject worship more of what God had for him to do in the way of loving service. He also knew that in the kingdom's eternity that he had before him, God would give him all that he wanted of worship, which was all that he wanted. For now, seasons of worship were enough, even with the dry times in between.

Revelation

There God was before him in the midst of the worshiping throng. He had come upon the worshipers unnoticed, joining them in the rear of their throng. Like every other kingdom resident, he worshiped God continually. He was conscious of God's presence at every moment and in every observation and activity. His continuous God-consciousness was not simply a matter of fact to him. Instead, it was a matter of complete satisfaction and celebration, indeed of utter veneration. In the kingdom, God-consciousness was instant, intimate, and familiar, no matter what he was at that moment doing. It meant continuously revering, honoring, and adoring God, again not as a matter of fact, labor, or discipline, as it might have been on earth, but more like a matter of sustenance and certainly a matter of joy. Removing that continuous worship would in the kingdom be like suffocating him. Yet at times, worship broke into celebratory throng. Residents simply gathered spontaneously to sing, dance, shout, and laugh, and even to murmur, whisper, and quietly squeal in worshiping joy. These times occasionally led to a special God appearance, although God was present at all times and even still somehow apparent at all times. In this special God appearance, the spectacular One suddenly rose out of and above the throng, as if a sleeping giant had suddenly awoken from slumber and stood up abruptly among them. The giant figure that suddenly arose from their worship in this instance seemed to bear every imaginable color and texture while taking on multiple different appearances and forms, so much so that he could once again not really describe God's image. God's appearance, though, caused the throng to emit roars of worship. Indeed, he, too, roared his worship from the rear of the throng that he had joined unnoticed. In this unusual instance, for every such instance seemed to be different, God responded with an uproarious laugh so low as to sound like rolling thunder. And then the moment was over, as spontaneously as it had arisen. The throng promptly dissipated, with he and each other individual resuming their own way, doubtless in individual worship.

Prayer

"Believe, and you will receive whatever you ask for in prayer." Matthew 21:22.

PRAYER

We adore you, Father, for prayer, for your desire to hear us and your willingness to answer. We would be nothing without the ability to communicate with you and without your readiness to respond. Without prayer, creation would isolate us from you rather than connect us to you. Without prayer, the world would hold us in a vast silence lacking consciousness, will, or heart. Prayer enlivens your universe, Father. Prayer makes you real and personal to us. Prayer gives us another way beyond your word to know and pursue your heart. We worship and esteem you for answering prayer, Father, for caring about our desires, requests, and thoughts. Without you answering our prayer calls, we would only be meditating, reflecting on your grandeur and awesome height. Your answers bring you down to us in the only way that a pure and holy God can come down, not by our command but by your gracious and merciful choice. That you, the holy One, deign to answer our prayers is fully enough for us to give you every possible praise. Prayer gives us purpose, prayer gives us hope, prayer gives us life, and in so giving, prayer gives us all the more reason to reverence, honor, and appreciate you, Lord, as the author of communication, reason, response, and life.

ANSWER

Your prayers come to me, my child, sibling to my Son, as welcome reverence. You have true cause to revere me, greater cause than you know, although you know enough to do as you should in honoring me. I especially welcome that you honor me for my willingness to engage with you in prayer. Too few of you pray as you should, which would be to pray without ceasing, knowing always that I answer. My kingdom is of course all around you. I act when you pray, and in my action I establish my reign and define the contours of my kingdom. See, my child, you should indeed pray, for in your prayer you enter my kingdom, that special place where I reside. Pagans carouse in wine, song, and dance, while you revel in prayer. In your prayer, my actions grow and my kingdom expands on earth, just as my kingdom is the expanse that is heaven. Keep adoring me for prayer, my praying child. Your adoration befits who I am. For you to adore me for prayer brings me closer to you while bringing you nearer to me. And because you have adored me for prayer, for my willingness to listen and respond, I am responding to you in blessing you with an ever greater commitment of my prayer-hearing ear. Pray for anything in the name of my beloved Son, and I will grant that which glorifies him, which will also bless you.

TRANSFORMATION

At first, prayer had seemed to her more like an obligation than an opportunity. She knew that Christians prayed and so she was to pray, but she had little sense of nearness to God and so little sense of her prayers being a conversation in which God heard and answered. Then, gradually, she had come to appreciate what prayer meant, not just answered prayer but the opportunity to pray knowing that God heard and responded. The realization that prayer was truly God conversation made her no more disciplined in prayer because to her relationship with God and the prayerful communication that relationship invited was simply not a discipline. Yet she found herself praying more often nonetheless, again not out of discipline but out of relationship. If, as she increasingly sensed, he was near, then she would be foolish not to acknowledge him and communicate with him. She began to have something akin to what she thought of as *chats* more so than formal prayers. Oh, she prayed dutifully from time to time, when called on to do so. And even without having formed a strict discipline of prayer, she still had some prayer habits that helped her to remember to pray. But more often than not, when she prayed, she did so spontaneously almost as if God had just walked into the room or otherwise appeared beside her. She liked this spontaneous kind of prayer. Indeed, she adored God for it. She liked having a present God and, although she felt the thought just a little surprising, suspected at the same time that God liked her presence.

REVELATION

She realized from her first moment that the kingdom solved instantly the significant issue that most everyone, she figured, faced with prayer. Was God really listening and responding? Of course, the kingdom, where God was always present, even if not always in instantiated form, could leave no doubt. The kingdom should, she had thought, make clear that God was listening and responding. Prayer, she would have thought, would not be the one-way communication that earth makes it seem to be. And indeed, the kingdom did make evident its residents' communication with God and God's communication back to the residents. Not, though, like she might have anticipated. What she promptly discovered was what she should have foreseen and predicted. God knows his people's minds, whether on earth or in the kingdom. In the kingdom, though, the residents know God's mind. She discovered that it was just as the scriptures had said that not only would God know her every thought, but that she also would see face to face and in doing so know fully. She couldn't exactly read God's mind, for who knows the mind of God other than the Son Jesus Christ? But she knew God's mind as God wished to reveal himself to her in intimate ongoing conversation. She dwelled entirely at all times with God. Prayer wasn't so much unnecessary in the kingdom as instead as if her interior dialogue was not with herself but directly with God. She knew his will intimately at all moments, sharing her thoughts continually as he shared his own. Prayer was no longer one-way communication but a continual embrace in rejoicing.

Eternity

"He has set eternity in the human heart." Ecclesiastes 3:11.

PRAYER

We cherish you, Father, for eternity. In eternity, you gave us an answer to the longing that every human heart has for more than temporary existence. When you gave us your consciousness, making us in your image, you also inevitably gave us knowledge of your pre-existence and eternity. In you, we conceive of the eternal, of you as the timeless originator before the origin of natural life. In you, we realize ceaseless life, perpetuity after natural life's end, even as we conceive of our own present fragility in imminent demise. You give us access to the eternal through the redemption and resurrection of your Son. Yet we do not want to live forever in these broken bodies in this broken world. The thought alone of eternal struggle in brokenness would crush our spirits today. So instead, after corrupt natural life, you promise us incorruptible supernatural life, eternally. In so doing, you give us the only answer that would satisfy our eternal souls while still lodged in mortal bodies. We cherish you because you hold all things not just for the moment but forever. We know that nothing and no one else is eternal except that you give everlasting life. You give your life unoriginated, inherent, and innate, and so welcome in relief of death so apparent. You alone are eternal, Father, and so you alone we worship.

ANSWER

You celebrate my eternity without knowing fully what eternity means. You are now only finite, while I am infinite, and the finite cannot fully know the infinite. You, though, will indeed taste eternity, once I transform you in resurrection and you enter my presence. Then, you will know more of what eternity means. If you knew now what eternity means, then you would not live as you do but would live as my Son lived among you, with the joy, power, and purpose of all who reside in my eternal kingdom. You are right, though, to dwell on my eternity, for from it you will draw much confidence to live as you are able until you join me in resurrection, just as my Son joined me in resurrection, even though he was with me before we created the world. The world is only temporary, but my kingdom is eternal. All who come to me will live with me throughout eternity, for my kingdom will come to the world, and my kingdom will not end like the world will end. Fix your eyes, then, on eternity. Do not see only what is temporary, but instead look beyond the temporary to my eternal. Because I am eternal, my kingdom is eternal, and all who are with me will also be eternal. And because you have looked to my eternity, I will fix eternity in your heart, and it will guide you in all things eternal.

TRANSFORMATION

He remembered having feared death when young for just the right reason that everyone should fear death, which lies in the annihilation of the soul. He no longer feared death, at least not that kind of fear of annihilation that gripped him occasionally when he was young. His only present fear of death was the natural fear that most everyone feels, in addition to annihilation's fear, which is the body's desire to go on living. He knew that he would, for instance, gasp for air if air were to deprive him. He knew that his body wanted to live, and he was glad for it because it meant that God desired him to continue for a time in natural vitality. Yet other than his body's natural desire to go on living, he had no fear of his natural demise because he had come to know that God would resurrect him in supernatural life just as God had resurrected Jesus. His confidence, of course, was not in his superiority or merit, knowing that he was neither superior nor meritorious, but instead entirely in God's grace and his own reliance on God's resurrected Son. He would live eternally, not in formulaic rescue as some suppose of Christian doctrine but in restored relationship. Nothing was more obvious to him now than that he would have once known God intimately and eternally as his creator, before the awful divorce. Nothing was more satisfying to him now than that he would once again know God intimately and eternally as his Savior, as soon as God determined was his time.

REVELATION

As with so many other aspects of the kingdom, he hadn't realized in advance how simply, elegantly, and purely the kingdom would resolve another of life's great questions. He had long wondered what eternity could possibly even mean to a person. Natural life impresses such a strong sense of passing time. Time has such a clear beginning and end. Life comes but just as surely goes, passing more and more quickly as one ages. He could not even comprehend eternal life. Surely the kingdom would have a lot to explore and every need met. But still, what would one do, forever? And who would one become, living forever? Yet once in the kingdom's eternity, he promptly realized that time's passing made no such sense. In the face of eternity, time didn't really come and go in earth-like linear fashion. Because eternity had no end, time lost to him all sense of passing. He realized in his first moments in the kingdom that indeed, in eternity, time is meaningless. He was simply present with God, which he realized was pretty much what Jesus had said in the scripture about the meaning of eternal life. Minutes, days, and hours did not pass. The first moment was just as present as the next. While he had memory, consciousness, and independence, just as he had on earth, he nonetheless now lived only in the present moment, not anticipating the future or dwelling on the past. All that God had for the kingdom would come to pass or again in some sense had already passed or was right then passing. He wasn't really living in the past or in the future, only in the present, but the present somehow included past and future, as if he was living in all at once. Events weren't so much happening seriatim as all at once. He was still experiencing only one event at a time but also seemed able to experience right then whichever event, past, present, or future, that he chose. Maybe that was how God knew even the future, that in the kingdom, time was eternal, and future was also present and past.

Divinity

"We clearly see God's divine nature from what he made." Romans 1:20.

PRAYER

We adore you, Father, for your divinity, for placing yourself above and beyond us, outside and over your creation as the immaculate and pre-existent creator. We would not worship a human hero, a mere mortal like us. We instead can only revere the celestial, heavenly, and divine. Thus, in your divinity, your apartness, numinosity, and otherworldliness, we gladly find all necessary and attractive cause for worship. Having made us little gods, with attributes of your own divinity, you have given us knowledge of your higher realm. You reveal to us a plain and presence beyond our direct perception, of which we yet have constant indications in the glitter, possibility, and providence of our own realm. How could we not pursue you, Father, reaching for your stars? Keep always before us your strange fearsomeness that evokes in us such deep and constant awe. Let us always shiver and quake in wonder before you, even as you invite us to intimacy, and you calm our anxiety, ease our insecurity, comfort us in affliction, and embrace us as yours. Show us just enough of your divinity, oh Father, to draw rather than repel us. Indeed, show us more of your Son in whom we bind both brother and thrall. We worship and cherish you in your divinity, Father, without which you would not be our God.

Answer

You indeed know me as divine, which is the only way to know a god of any kind, although in knowing me you know the one true God, for you have none other to know than me. I am the only transcendent One, outside of all that you know. You know me only through what I created, meaning that you know me only as I show myself to you. You will never be fully as I am, even though you are my image, because as your creator and the creator of all that you know, I am beyond what any of my creation can fully know. You rightly quake in creature fear at my otherworldliness. I desire that you do so, not because fear feeds me but because in your fear you show that you know who I am, what I have done, and what I will do. Only in your holy fear can you draw near to me, as a young child draws near to a parent only in showing that the parent knows what the child cannot yet know and controls what the child cannot yet control. You are not intimate with me as equals are intimate but as the subordinate are intimate with the one on whom they depend for everything. Your salvation is not in grasping my goodness but instead in utter dependence on it. Your standing is not in assuming my authority but instead in utter submission to it. My divinity is not yours, making all the more fitting that you revere it. And because you honor my divinity, I will reveal more of it to you in the days and years ahead, even while you remain fixed and finite in your natural being. As you see more of my divinity, so will you also see more of your need of me, which sight will bless you.

Transformation

She had come fairly early in her life to the point of knowing her need to acknowledge the divine. Her realization was something that many never come to know while too many others learn only quite late in life. She had always had the same sense that most others have of the world being larger or perhaps stranger than it daily reveals. She hadn't pursued magic or the occult, fantasy or science fiction, or even the extraordinary wonders that terrestrial science and astrophysics suggested, although she could sense the supernatural in those and other things. Nor had personal miracles confronted her as she knew that they had confronted and changed others, although she did have the remarkable record of the Bible. The Bible was certainly a large part of her wonder, especially in its record of Jesus's many extraordinary miracles and in his resurrection, God's greatest miracle of them all. Yet somehow, she had the sense that even without the Bible's historicity, she felt that she would have come to the point of knowing God's divinity. She had no place for a world without the divine. God had quite evidently formed her heart and soul to know him. Oh, she could have rejected him, she knew quite well. He had given her just enough will that she could have believed herself independent, a creature of chance adrift in a flat world. She knew, though, that her life wasn't anything of the sort. She was both a product and ward of the divine, and glad for it.

REVELATION

She gradually came to realize that divinity permeated the kingdom, imbuing its every minute facet with the glorious reflection of God. Although the kingdom had many appearances like earth, the kingdom was of course simultaneously utterly distinct. God's pure presence, which sin no longer veiled or mediated, made all the difference, that much she knew. Yet the realization that God's presence changed everything about the kingdom took her a little while to make, like adjusting one's eyes to bright light. She almost had to shield herself, a mental sort of covering of the eyes, until she could take in more of the kingdom's God reflection. The mirror of his divinity was simply everywhere. His divinity's mirror was in the smiles of the other residents and the curl of every leaf on every bush or tree. Reminders and reflections of God's glory were in every sense impression, including sight, sound, smell, touch, and taste, that the kingdom offered her. She delighted in every such sense impression. She had for a time tried to gauge gently how much she could ingest without her senses overwhelming her mind. But after a while, she learned to trust that God overwhelming her with his reflection was just fine. Indeed, she learned to embrace those many moments when she just stopped in his irresistible awe. Divinity was no enemy but an utter friend. On earth she had protected herself against everything, both seeming good and seeming evil, trying to hold her sanity in the balance. In the kingdom, she could abandon herself to everything and anything because all was God. She had no need for holding things tight within her mind and soul, guarding her senses. She could instead drink constantly and deeply from every kingdom offer because every offer was God.

Glory

"We have seen his glory, the glory of the one and only Son." John 1:14.

PRAYER

We revere you, Father, for your glory. We worship you for the glory that you gave to your Son for us to see and to which we may witness. You would be a different God if you had no glory, nothing to attract us to you, astonish us with your wonder, and make us want to shout in exultation and victory. The weight of your glory is both vast and yet somehow also light and luminous. Your glory is at once so incomprehensibly burdensome as to shatter our pretensions and yet still so light as to draw us upward toward you. The best part of us hungers for your glory, wishing to partake of it only in the sense of rejoicing and exulting along with it, not pretending to either add or detract. Your glory imbues the world, without being in the world, just enough to let us know that you are still here, still governing, still providing, still inviting. We want to bask and revel in your glory, oh Lord. Our hearts long for your radiance, wishing just once more to taste of it that it might melt every hardness and remove every dross. Your glory leads, your glory feeds, your glory reveals, your glory renews. Father, we give you all glory, we worship none other than you and your Son. Let us continue to cherish your magnificence and grandeur that so permeates, suffuses, and vitalizes this otherwise dreary world. Show yourself anew, Father, that we might praise you.

ANSWER

I desire that you witness my glory as you do, even if you now see my glory only in shadow, as you must presently do. You cannot see more of my glory until my Spirit has prepared you because to see more of my glory would so astonish you as to harm you. I have hidden you thus in my Son, on whom you can look without harm, indeed with healing. My Spirit carries my Son's image to you in ways that you can understand and embrace without astounding and shattering you. He mediates my glory for you. Continue your embrace of him. For now, draw from him, feed from him, and renew yourself from him. Know, though, that we have more glory to show you when your transformation is complete and you have entered my kingdom, as my Son returned to my kingdom. For him, I lifted the ancient gates of glory. He has shown you the same way through, which is in him, taking on his redemptive image for you. You have no other way to see my full glory than to follow my Son who saw my glory and is my glory. In my kingdom, all is glory, suffused of my presence, shining without sun. You will drink of my river of life, that which flows from my glory throughout my kingdom, where none has any glory but me and the one with whom I share my glory. And because you witness and embrace my glory, my Spirit will share with you, and with those followers whom you also embrace, more of the glory of my Son until my Spirit draws all of you.

TRANSFORMATION

He had read and read, and heard and heard, of the glory of God while only yet barely sensing what that glory must mean. Then he saw an earthly vision of it, a portrayal of what fully facing the glory might be like. His earthly vision was of that mind-shattering moment when nothing mediates the glory of God and one must do nothing other than sing glorious song. God gave him other tastes of it, each so sweet that he knew that God must stop those tastes lest they cause him to abandon any other purpose than the pursuit of more of them. No narcotic could induce equal ecstasy. God's glory remained pure and apart from him, not induced within him but rather shown to him, touching him, yes, but remaining supernatural and pure despite its encounter with the natural and corrupt. Where God's glory touched, it transformed. He thereafter felt as if a golden presence burned secretly within him, to which he might turn at any moment, when for that moment all again would be God, with nothing else mattering. He wondered for a time what to do with the mind-shattering light to which he could turn in thrall but in the end decided not to seek it often or to abuse it. In fact, he felt the Spirit cautioning him that the event meant nothing other than that he had once seen a very small part of the immeasurably large glory of God. Seek God, he concluded, seek God in Christ. The glory was the allure, but the reward was in Christ.

REVELATION

He soon realized that God's glory, like God's divinity, suffused the kingdom. The kingdom was not merely otherworldly and pure, as he knew that divinity must be. The kingdom also held a magnificence and grandeur befitting the God of glory. The kingdom reflected God's glory differently than it did God's divinity. The kingdom mirrored God's divinity constantly, in everything large and small. Nothing was corrupt, all instead pure. He could not see, touch, taste, or smell anything without having an instant sense of its divine perfection. On the other hand, God's glory, his magnificence, seemed to arise in swells. Divine perfection supplied the necessary tableau or foundation for those swells of glory. Although it at first seemed to him impossible, the kingdom soon confirmed for him that God was greater than perfect. God was also glorious beyond his perfection. The kingdom showed him God's swelling glory in various great displays, some anticipated and others spontaneous. Some displays simply involved spectacular vistas, like the towering snow-capped mountain ranges that appeared at times on the horizon or the glassy seas glinting with diamond-like light. Other displays suggested glory's enormous heart, like the time that the Son of God walked in the form of a huge and regal lion through a pristine valley. Still other swells of glory involved incomprehensible revelations of awesome form, breathtaking sound, and brilliant light. He would on earth have mistaken these displays as spectral apparitions, when in the kingdom they were each obviously entirely real. The displays were not calculated or purposeful in timing and arrangement, as if to impress the kingdom's residents. They were plainly instead God's glory simply bursting forth from his own nature. Indeed, the displays occurred whether or not the kingdom's residents happened to observe and appreciate them, which of course they always and deeply did. While glory didn't suffuse the kingdom, glory elevated it beyond its divine perfection. God resided in the kingdom in his full glory, which was ready at all times to burst forth. He came quickly to know just how much more special that glory made the already-perfect and entirely divine place.

Sovereignty

"How long, Sovereign Lord, until you judge?" Revelation 6:10.

PRAYER

We revere you, Father, for your sovereignty. We are so relieved that you alone decide whom to increase or decrease, elevate or diminish, accept or reject. You do as you will, subject to none, controlled by none.

You are our ultimate authority, above all, over all, ruling all. You stand alone, while to you every knee bows. You are not of one tribe or another, not marked, limited, or confined by culture, affinity, ethnicity, ancestry, or race. Nothing defines you other than your own words and actions, and the Son whom you honor in what you and he say and do. When leaders do not guide us, we recruit and elevate harsh masters hoping that they will conquer and subjugate us, controlling in us the excesses in which we engage due to our rebel nature. Yet we do not need these masters. We instead need you as sovereign God. We need your sovereignty and lordship like we need food and water, light and breath. In our corruption, we would not survive without governance and subjection. We need one who is greater than us and greater than all, to whom we and our friends and enemies must turn or will fall. Unlike our worldly rulers, you do not depend on history, politics, power, alliance, or connivance. Your ascendancy is unique in that you rule ordained and divine. Judge us swiftly and mercifully, oh Lord, under the mantle of your Son, for if anyone else were to measure our merit, we would fall forever condemned. Do not let us fall into the hands of earthly rulers, none of whom know your mercy. We cherish your sovereignty, Father, for you alone rule as merciful King of kings.

ANSWER

Indeed, I rule as sovereign, for I am without beginning and without end. None preceded me, and none will outlast me. No one can contradict my truth because I am reason itself, holding all things together. No one proves me wrong, for I created all things and thus hold the keys to proof. Every one of my acts stands alone as sovereign, finding its only basis in my creation and my attributes, and thus only in me. I am the measure of all things, including you who stand with me and those who attempt to stand against me but must therefore fall. A sovereign has the power to share the sovereign's rule, which I have done with my one and only Son. He is my begotten who listens to me and does only my will, and so I listen to him because he speaks what I desire him to say. We are your sovereign, your ruler, and in our merciful desire also your rescue. We do not rule to oppress and destroy as your earthly rulers prefer to rule. Instead, we save, elevate, and protect you, to give you the life for which we created you in my Son's image. We do as we wish, but our desire is for your devotion, that you would love as we do. And because you have cherished my sovereignty, I will listen to your appeals to my sovereignty. You will have all things that you ask in my will and my beloved Son's name.

Transformation

In their household, they knew God as sovereign and treated him as such. They hadn't always done so. They had taken some time to grow together in the knowledge, wisdom, and pursuit of the Lord. As is so often the case with households, challenges taught them more about the Lord's sovereignty than blessings had taught, although both were good teachers. They learned that because the Lord had made all things, all things operated for the good of the one who followed the Lord. One cannot live in his kingdom and expect to prosper under one's own rules. The Lord rules, they knew. The more that they admitted his sovereignty and bent to his merciful rule, the more that they treasured his dominion, power, control, and rule. They had known other masters, earthly masters for whom they had toiled under hard rule. They had also known idols for which they had toiled without reward and without rule. And so they had turned from earthly masters, other than those whom the Lord appointed. They turned also from idols, having learned that none were worth the toil and none capable of merciful rule. What they most appreciated having learned, though, was that they needed God's rule. They knew that without a ruler, they were lost not only to the world but from one another. God's sovereignty had knit them together in just the way of his kind rule. Submit happily to his rule, they had together long concluded.

Revelation

The kingdom instantly satisfied another large earthly concern that she had hardly realized that she'd had. She had seldom if ever been sure just who was in charge, whom to obey, what authority others had or didn't have, and what instruction and course to follow. She had often felt that if only she knew the reliable protocol, policy, or instruction, then she could simply follow it, and outcomes would be alright. Yet on earth, that clarity was hardly ever present. No one was sovereign. Everyone and everything seemed subject to vagary, caprice, and whim. No one seemed properly in charge, and so none could ever relax. She, of all people, certainly wasn't in control, and nor did she particularly want to be. She nonetheless in some strange way had hungered for authority because no one seemed properly to rule. In the kingdom, she instantly found that authority. The kingdom ordered everything according to God's complete and perfect sovereignty. No one other than God ruled, and God ruled perfectly. God's sovereignty made itself evident in the largest matters, such as when corporate worship commenced and crescendoed, and in the smallest matters, such as when she might sit for her own silent intimate worship. She knew what God wanted, from whom, and where and when, as did every other kingdom resident. Extraordinarily but understandably, and to her great satisfaction, God's utter rule did not make her chafe in the least or feel any less at liberty. Rather, she relaxed and reveled in knowing his every request, desire, and command. Earth's subtly but grossly disruptive confusion was gone. In the kingdom, no one was in charge other than God. The kingdom's revelation had instantly and simply solved another bewildering and besetting earthly problem, for which she now felt great relief, even though she had hardly realized that she had for so long carried such a great burden.

Locality

"You fill me with joy in your presence." Psalm 16:11.

PRAYER

We cherish you, Father, for your locality. We adore how you are both there and everywhere, and yet also here, present, near, located proximate to us in time and place. You would be a different god, indeed a lesser god, and not our one great God at all, if you were not wholly present with us. You have located yourself in our corner, district, and vicinity as we face enemies and embrace friends, suffer sickness and rejoice in health. What a precious God you are, Father, that you are not merely a force, theory, or mist. How precious that you are not merely an overseer outside and above what you create, nor merely a concept, construct, or set of principles. Instead, you exist personified so as to inhabit your creation. You make yourself real to us in every sense that you made us real to ourselves and to one another, doing so in particular through your glorious Son. You were always proximate and present, both here and there, acting in one region while also in another, always local, concerned, and involved. You then sent your Son as Emanuel, confirming yourself forever as the God who was and is *with* his people. In doing so, you proved yourself to us as personal, present, authentic, extant, and existent. You summon us to you through your Son, ushering us once again into your presence, that proximity that heals and within which we worship. We would be nothing, oh Father, without your presence, without the privilege of walking with your Spirit and kneeling before you on your holy ground.

ANSWER

You know and love me as God because I revealed myself to you in my Son. I wanted you to know me through my Son because doing so would give you ground on which to fix the devotion that I seek from you. I came to you in him so that you could come to me through him. I created you fixed and local, capable of knowing only the fixed and local. And so in my love for you, I made myself fixed and local in my Son so that you could know me in the only way that you can know anyone, as incarnate. Know me as you know my Son, for that is why I gave him to you, that you would live in devotion to me through him. I am real, just as my Son is real and my Spirit is real. You can only know me if you first know that I am real, that I exist before you and in you, and that you live in me and through me. You love me because you know that I am, just as I said that I am and my Son also said that he is and was with me. He was with me in the beginning. We have always been. Your devotion is so sure because you know that we exist. You know that my Son came, did as I asked, and returned to me. You know, too, that I sent my Spirit to you. You have my Spirit in you, and you are in my Spirit. My Spirit lives as I live and my Son lives. And because you adore me in person, because I am near and my Spirit is near, I will reveal ever more of myself to you through my Spirit. You need only to continue to listen to my Spirit whose role remains to reveal me to you. Adore me as you would adore the holy One who comes to you.

TRANSFORMATION

She held a growing sense that God was very near. He had at times seemed distant, but those times were past, long past, and had been only her imagination. He now was near, as he had always been near. Only now she could sense his proximity, nearly as if she felt his breath on her, warming her when she was cold and cooling her when she was warm. She needed his nearness, cherished his proximity. She trusted now that he was not just real but also personal to her, friend to her, even while fully Lord to her. He not only kept her in awe of him, holy fear of him, but also kept her in thrall of him, looking to him, admiring him, wanting more of his presence. Even as she wanted his presence, she knew that he would come to her, reveal more of himself to her, as her desire for him grew. He made no game of her desire, did not keep himself from her. Rather, she knew that he was drawing her to him in the only way that she could reach him in his holiness, gradually, in purifying her of all things that kept her from him. She could only draw nearer by letting go of things that held her back from him. And so she kept letting go, kept learning to trust him that he would hold her, protect her, provide for her, and draw her to him. He was coming to her, and this time, she would not be letting him go.

Revelation

She had often wondered how the kingdom would resolve her desire to be constantly close to her Lord. She was confident, as the scriptures seemed to promise, that in the kingdom she would not suffer that kind of aching longing for her Lord. No more tears, the scriptures reassured. She didn't have long to wait for her answer. The moment that the kingdom opened fully to her, she met and embraced the Lord. What, after all, had the scriptures said that the kingdom meant, other than to be with the Lord in his paradise? She couldn't say later how long their embrace had lasted. Perhaps it had lasted for an eternity. All that she knew was that once having fell into his instant embrace, she hadn't ever really let him go. Nor had he let her go. Kingdom life was life in the Lord's embrace. His love filled every bit of her for every moment of her eternal residence. Their long embrace slowly removed her decades of earthly longing while healing her decades of earthly loss. Their embrace must also have accomplished for her a thousand other things that needed his love's resurrection. In time, though, she hadn't any longer the sense of their literal embrace, for which she had hoped so earnestly and that she had very much needed at her first kingdom entry. Because he was still with her in every respect, as he always would be, she only realized that they were no longer embracing when he swept one of his arms wide showing her, indeed gifting to her, every grandeur of his glorious kingdom. The kingdom's King would have many more literal embraces for her, as often and as for long as she desired. He would also share his perfect love fully and effectively with her in each embrace. Those embraces gave her every good comfort and reassurance to accept his invitation to enjoy the full grandeur of the kingdom. He was, of course, that grandeur, the One who would never leave her and never forsake her.

2
Confession

"If we confess our sins, then he will forgive and purify us." 1 John 1:9.

To you, Father, we confess our propensity toward doing wrong. We admit that we are so often wrought wrong in this broken and corrupt state that we find ourselves. We are indeed wretched, pitiful, poor, blind, and naked. Our sins are so common because they are both of commission, our doing outright wrongs, and also of omission, our failing to do right such that wrong prevails. Each of them, both commission and omission, we know to be equal iniquity. We know fully our corrupt condition, living in it moment to moment, day to day, so much so that we feel natural and at home in our sodden state. Yet we do not want our wickedness to keep you from hearing us, approaching us, living with us, letting us serve and worship you. We recognize and admit that corruption separates us from you, creating a chasm between us over which you will not come, see, or hear. You cannot countenance evil, and so you would leave us in our sin except that you love us so intensely. And so you look at us and hear us the only way that you can stand, which is through the perfectly merciful image of your willingly sacrificial Son. When we confess the evil that we cherish in our hearts and turn from wickedness to your mediating Son, you hear us again, answering every prayer within your will. Father, we are contemptible in your sight but clothed completely in the radiance of your redeeming Son. Hear our prayers of confession.

Doubt

"Pleasing God is impossible without faith." Hebrews 11:6.

PRAYER

We confess our doubt to you, Father. We admit that we have times when we hardly acknowledge that you exist. We confess that in some of those times, we question, however briefly, whether you really do exist. Why would you ever favor us when we pretend that you are not even here to grant us your favor? Our greatest affront to you is not disobedience, which would at least admit your authority and standard, even if to attempt to avoid both. Instead, our greatest affront to you is to imagine that you are not, when you indubitably are. We may as well deny ourselves as deny you, when we know that we cannot ourselves deny. One who does not exist cannot deny existence. Yet we still deny you when we have even less standing to do so than to deny our own existence. How can the creature deny the creator? We certainly know that we did not make this place, nor did we make ourselves. We still so often act as though we did both, create this place and ourselves. In so acting, we deny ourselves as creatures while denying you as creator. We are oblivious to you, without thought of you, ignorant of your will and action. We breathe as if breath is our own when instead you could without notice take breath from us and in so doing take our lives. You protect, provide, bless, and enliven, while we think all of it to be of our own doing. When we do turn to you, we act as if you might not even be there. We distrust your generosity and disbelieve in your care, when we have constant evidence of both all around us. You published your plan for us and then gave it spectacular evidence, and yet we hesitate to think the concrete and visible to be real. Father, forgive our lack of belief, for which we have no cause and nothing but contrary evidence, and instead give us faith.

ANSWER

You should first know that I embrace deep, honest, heartfelt, and authentic confession. Know, too, that you confess wisely in first admitting your doubt of me, as long as you then turn away from your doubt and to acknowledging me. No one who doubts that I exist will have my favor. To converse in prayer with me, to commune with me and receive my favor, you must first believe that I exist, as even demons so believe. When you doubt, you purport to deny me, when I am the One whom none can deny. I always was, I am now, and I always will be, whether or not you, many, few, or anyone at all believes that I exist. Your imaginings are unimportant to me. I make you, while none make me. I, not you, decide who will be and who will not be. As the author of all life and of each life, only I can deny that any will exist or not exist. I welcome your confession of doubt because none can genuinely confess to me without knowing that I exist. Continue to confess in earnest of your doubt of me, while asking of me that you no longer doubt. I will then show you ever greater evidence of me until you no longer doubt but know that I am your God and always will be God of all who ever exist. I do not reveal myself to those who doubt but to those who know that I am and in that sure knowledge of me ask ever greater evidence of me. I appear to those who seek and desire me, not those who shun and abhor me. Your confession draws my notice and with my notice draws more of me.

TRANSFORMATION

He had no cause to doubt. God had certainly never given him any such grounds but had instead long loved, guarded, and guided him. Yet his faith found its seed in his confession of doubt. As he trusted in God but confessed his doubt, God then gave him reason to see. His doubt didn't fade by denying doubt as much as in confessing doubt and receiving God's wisdom with which to banish it. As he confessed to God more, God consoled, counseled, and guided him more. In so doing, he began to see that confessing to God was like a young child admitting fears to its parent, giving the parent reason to reassure along with proof of protection. In time, though, God had supplied such evident reassurance so often that he no longer really doubted. Instead, he could turn his questions away from whether God existed and cared, to whether God's care extended all the way to resurrection. He knew then that he had abundant inspired evidence with which to extinguish his doubt of God. Jesus, after all and above all, had attested to the Father. Why would he any longer doubt, when to doubt would be to call Jesus a liar? Matthew, Mark, Luke, John, Peter, James, Paul, and many others had also witnessed to God in Christ's resurrection. Indeed, in doing so, they had faced their own death. God thus answered his confession. He had the miracle of eternal life, his heart having believed. A great cloud of witnesses had convinced his inquiring mind. With God's grace and mercy, he had matured beyond doubt.

REVELATION

The kingdom, he realized, was a completely alien place, indeed a completely forbidden place, for the many kinds of sin that on earth had bothered and in some instances beset him. The most obvious of those banished sins was doubt. Above all sins, the kingdom made doubt impossible. God was as real as, no *more* real than, anything in the kingdom, the entirety of which made clear that God was its sole creative source. In the kingdom, one could not doubt that God existed when God sat high, living, and active on his throne right in front of every resident. Indeed, not long after his arrival, he had the great fortune of having God give him an extraordinary opportunity to see just how unreal doubt was—and how harmful. In a brief moment of reflection, he had the privilege of God granting that he should momentarily observe across the vast chasm a God-denier whom death had won against Christ's invitation. The pitiful man, mired in frigid dark slime and utterly blind, strained as if to look painfully up. If he would have had any sight, which he plainly did not, then he would not have looked up at heaven but instead at a low black stalactite-covered ceiling off which acids dripped like steaming rain into the frigid mire. He could hear the man muttering curses at his condition, curses that at once railed against God while at the same time mocking and denying God's existence, in just the way that those who refuse God's love both rail and deny simultaneously, irrationally. Oddly, though, the man seemed more robotic than human in nature, even though clearly still flesh rather than mechanical. The mired man seemed no longer to have any will or mind. Instead, dark figures fed him the vile words that he spat out alternately as epithets against and denials of God. Fortunately, the privileged observation dissipated nearly as quickly as God had granted it, leaving him fully restored in the glorious confidence, grace, and mercy of the very obviously extant God. God reigned, he was so enormously glad. God's kingdom permitted no denial. Denials were illusion, while God was real.

Motives

"You ask with wrong motives to pursue your pleasures." James 4:3.

PRAYER

We confess that too many of our requests of you, Father, too many of our prayers and petitions, are for our own pursuits rather than in your will for us. We seek pleasure when we should seek to please you, when we should seek to do your will. We ask for things that would serve and please us rather than ask for things that would serve and please you. Father, forgive us for wanting you to make our lives pleasurable, for wanting you to satisfy our senses and sensuality rather than to satisfy us with you. Reveal to us our self-seeking, the ways in which we pursue our pastimes and recreations simply to fill longings that instead only you can fill. Show us the difference between our pleasure seeking and our seeking your pleasure. Help us to trust that when we seek your pleasure and pursue your will, we receive the blessing that we cannot pursue directly without affront to you. We ask with wrong motives, moved only by another moment's fancy, seeking amusements that must look capricious and whimsical to you. Motivate us instead to discern and embrace your will, Father, even as you forgive our selfish motives in petitioning you. Give us your heart in order that we would seek your will, and then we will pray with right motives. We do not receive because we ask with wrong motives, and so we turn away from our own motives to the motives that please you.

ANSWER

Your motives are not my motives. Nor are your motives holy motives, righteous motives, beneficial motives under which you and your family would flourish. Your motives lead you to death, whereas my desire for you is life, which is why I command that you submit your stubborn will to my beneficial will for you. You know me and know my love for you. Unlike those who openly reject me, your struggle is not to know the right way, which you know is my way. You have confessed your love for my Son and your need of his sacrifice and redemption. You know also of his resurrection in which you will find eternal life. Your struggle is instead to commit your stubborn will to me. Your head knows to follow me, but your heart deceives you into following your own desires. Know then that you must give your heart to me, not just have your mind commit and mouth confess to me. You must examine your heart as I probe your heart, which is to banish from it all devotion other than that which you give to me. Devote your heart solely to me. Then I will show you more of my will for you, and you will follow my will, glorifying me. In glorifying me, you will find that satisfying purpose, identity, and meaning that you crave because I gave it to you as your gift when I created you. You crave because I placed desire for me within you. Align your will to mine, and I will satisfy that which you crave. You have no satisfaction other than satisfaction in me. I alone satisfy you because I made you for me. And because you have confessed your corrupt motives, I will give you a new heart for me and satisfy all that you desire.

TRANSFORMATION

She had always had a passion for things, just like she knew others had their passions. Providentially, she had learned early in life that she could not satisfy that passion in the way that the world offered her. She could spend herself in pursuit of her passions and yet not mollify or placate them, no less fulfill them. She had instead learned that she must link those passions with the will of her Lord for her, or her pursuits, whether or not achieved, would leave her tired, weakened, and empty. She gradually found richness, a dreamlike and otherworldly sort of peace and fulfillment, in pursuits that seemed at once to be her own desires and the desires of her Lord for her. If she was not striving with the Lord, then her striving exhausted her. Yet when she had examined her heart so fully as to rid of it everything other than her love for him, her heart then seemed to lead her to just the right skillful devotion. Sometimes that devotion entailed prayer in solitude, while other times studies and reflection, and still other times whirlwinds of service activities or even raucous worship and joyful fellowship. What surprised her was that she found such welcome variety in her devotion to the Lord's will. The Lord did not desire just one thing but all things that he created her to offer. She could alternately pray, study, reflect, create, serve, laugh, sing, and worship, and both move and hold still, and change and stay the same, all in the Lord's will for her. And in so doing, her life took a shape that she had not anticipated or planned. Her life was so increasingly rich, even if stilled filled with frequent challenges, that she just kept letting go of her own will to accept more of the Lord's will for her. She had found the right motives, and they were his motives.

REVELATION

She soon discovered that the kingdom relieved another one of her many earthly quandaries, things that she had hardly realized weighed her down so heavily. Kingdom life had turned out to be as much a process of the unburdening of sin's earthly cares and worries, as of embracing God's full glory. Neither unburdening nor embrace, of course, could happen without the other. She could not give God his full celestial embrace without first letting go of her old terrestrial anxieties. Anxiety over motives turned out to be a primary example. She hadn't in her former life grasped just how besetting was the question of why, or for whom, she should desire and do things. Once in the kingdom, though, she could both discern from her clarity of mind and feel from the lightness of her step and spirit just how burdensome that old question had been. Her every kingdom thought and action just naturally, or perhaps supernaturally, had God's glory as motive. She had no need, God continuously fulfilling all need, and so she had no reason for selfish motive. She had no desire beyond God's utterly satisfying embrace, and so she had no motive to pursue her own desire. She had perfect liberty, even more so than ever on earth, but she also had perfect will, wholly to please God. In the kingdom, the thought of having any other motive simply had no rational basis. One cannot start a rational thought from the standpoint of the world upside down. Because everything so plainly proceeded from and to the glory of God, motive had only one direction. She had an infinite variety of choices still to make, but all of those kingdom options aligned perfectly with the generous will of God. Who had any need for any other motive? Kingdom life clarified and purified all motive into one.

Greed

"Be on your guard against all kinds of greed." Luke 12:15.

PRAYER

Father, forgive us for our greed. Forgive us for our endless pursuit of more of anything that might please us in our many insatiable desires. We are voracious in our appetites, never satisfied, always hungry and pursuing. We not only pursue but also obtain, acquire, and accumulate. Even when we are full, we feel fullness not to be enough. We always want more, when we already have more than enough and even when we know or suspect that more will hurt us. As we pile up pleasures and conceits, they do no more than increase our insecurity while decreasing our satisfaction and contentment. These selfish and destructive pursuits reflect our ingrained greed, Father, a twisted condition at our core that shows our incomplete self without you who completes us. This greed we know comes from our fruitless attempt to fulfill by our own stealth labor or deceit what only you can fulfill. We are greedy because we turn from you who would satisfy that desire from which greed emanates but greed cannot content. We know that we have all in you. Father, forgive us for our greed, gluttony, and appetite. Turn us to you, and fill us anew in order that greed would no longer entice. We know that you alone suffice.

ANSWER

You confess rightly when you confess your greed. Your greed is like the greed of all others. Greed is common among you. You have the same corruption that others share because every one of you shares the same corrupt nature. You confess rightly because you cannot reform your corrupt nature without me. I am your only salvation from greed, just as I am your only salvation from every other corruption that stains and destroys you. Corruption is in your nature, and only I can give to you a new nature. Indeed, in your confession, you have taken on my nature in the image of my Son and influence of my Spirit. You have new life in my Spirit, with your old greedy self having died if you will only accept it, which you have done in your confession. Keep confessing to me your insatiable appetite, and I will keep turning your appetite toward feasting on my Son. You will assume his flesh and image even as his blood washes you of corruption. You confess rightly but still do not know the depths of your need for confession. My Spirit will continue to show you where your greed has come to my attention. When my Spirit does so, confess your greed quickly in order that I do not hold it against you and withdraw from you any part of my provision. If you pursue your greed, acquiring where you should not purchase and hoarding where you have no need, then nothing will satisfy you. If you pursue your greed, then your hunger will return, increase, and become like an unquenchable fire to you, destroying your soul and spirit. Guard therefore against greed lest it consume you as it has consumed so many others. And if you continue to guard against greed through honest confession, then I will reward your humility with a bounty that you had not expected and of the type that satisfies rather than ignites ever-greater hunger.

Transformation

He had no real passionate desires to acquire and accumulate. Indeed, he instead understood the danger of greed and the opposite value of contentment. Strangely, though, he nonetheless kept recognizing within himself both small and large instances of greed. He knew that the Spirit brought to him each such recognition. On each such occasion, he thanked the Spirit, confessed to the Father his greed, and in the Son's name asked that the Father would take greed from him. He didn't do these things out of formula or function but instead because he wanted a heart for God rather than for anything approximating fame or fortune. In that way, he knew that greed was at once both his problem, just as greed is everyone's problem, but also not his problem, in that the Spirit warned him against greed, which he quickly confessed. While he knew that these things were difficult to judge, he nonetheless felt that over the very long term, his greed had, if not disappeared, then at least changed in scope and character. He seemed somehow still to be greedy but not about the same things and perhaps not to the same degree, although even feeling so, he was not in the least ready to let down any part of his guard against greed. He knew that the one who sees in himself no greed is the one whom greed is most likely to consume secretly. Better, he figured, that he knew his natural self to be just as it always was including in its deceptiveness. Yet the odd thing was that even as he sensed that he might in his spirit be a little less greedy than before, he seemed somehow to have acquired greater riches, not necessarily earthly riches, but riches nonetheless. He carried with him a sense of security and accomplishment that really had little or nothing to do with the false security that the world offers or the world's false sense of accomplishment. God seemed to have answered his prayer for relief from greed both by quelling the false desire while also providing his own bounty that satisfies.

Revelation

He saw early that the kingdom dealt in its own way with the desires of its residents. Kingdom life had not removed from him the sense of desire. He continued to desire God in his wondrous dimensions, Father, Son, and Holy Spirit. He continued to desire every expression of God's love and glory, just as God continually offered them in both predictable and surprising form. What the kingdom had promptly removed, though, was *unfilled* desire. The kingdom simply did not leave him wanting. He could drink in whatever much or little God provided of anything and instantly find it wholly fulfilling because it came from God. He could then desire again, once again to find fulfillment from the first offer of God's provision. Desire thus never met its earthly corollaries in unfilled want and frustration. Unmet need could never coagulate into greed and hoarding. The kingdom unburdened him of his former abode's gnawing sense of wanting to hold onto things or experiences lest he not get enough of them then or next time. He no longer had any need for grasping, storing, and protecting. Rather, he had continually to let every experience and every acquisition promptly go again in order to receive God's next generous and fully satisfying offer. In the kingdom, to hold onto anything, as he would formerly have tried often to do, was to receive *less* rather than *more*. The kingdom's God economy was utterly unlike the transactional economy on earth because of its boundless bounty. Everything proceeded in an endlessly rich circle from God and to God, eliminating even the possibility of greed.

Fear

"'Do not fear, for I am with you.'" Isaiah 41:10.

PRAYER

Father, we confess to you our weak-willed, anxious, timorous fear. We admit how we fail to take heart and trust and rely on you. You say repeatedly not to fear, and yet we do fear and not soundly but instead cravenly. Our only fear should be fear of you, reverential fear, fear of your splendor overcoming us or, indeed true fear, of facing eternal consequence without your splendor. In that reverential fear, we would simply obey you, clinging to your Son. Your promise in your perfect love would defeat our every opponent and overcome our every challenge. You would remove all fear from us, replacing fear with courage and confidence. Yet instead we fear cowardly, dreading that we must face only that which you call, equip, and discipline us to engage, rout, and conquest. If we did not have you on whom to rely, then we would fear justly, for any lethal enemy could without notice overtake and destroy us. Their threats would be real. We could then hide in our bare-subsistence work as Gideon did before you called him, waiting for the enemy to steal from us what little we had to sustain us. Instead, though, we have you on whom to rely, you who defeat all challengers, you in whom we have the promise of eternal life as your own sons and daughters. Still, we fear, fearing even punishment and even so little as insult and humiliation. In doing so, in giving way to fear, we disgrace and abandon you. Father, forgive us for our abundant fears, fears for which we have no cause when you protect us. Then help us to overcome those fears.

ANSWER

How indeed, when in my care, can you fear anything other than the loss of me? You know that I will hold and protect you forever. Did I not resurrect my Son? Does he not rule at my right hand, while having given himself in order that you would not perish but instead have eternal life with me? I have promised you eternal life for having trusted in my Son's glorious salvation. He wrought your salvation at my behest for my glory and the glory that I would bestow on him. You know that you have no need to fear, having acknowledged my Son's gift and in doing so received my eternal life. Your fear evidences only your failure to trust entirely in me. When you fear, you deny me, which is why I tell you not to fear. Do not deny me, and you will not fear. Trust in me, and your fear will abate. In its stead, courage will arise in you. Whatever you face is temporary, whereas I am eternal, and in me you also are eternal. Do not sacrifice the eternal for the temporary. Hold on to the eternal, while enduring the temporary. The things that you fear last only for a time, while my salvation lasts for eternity. You have no need to fear because I have loved you, and my love is greater than death. So because you have confessed your fear while asking me to relieve you of it, I will do that which relieves you of fear, which is to remind you of your salvation and your eternal life with me. You will not fear but instead have the confidence of your conviction. You have committed yourself to me in trusting my offer of my Son, and so I will care for you eternally.

TRANSFORMATION

She knew fear, indeed just the kind of fear that she knew that God detested. She had taken a long time to realize that her fear was something that God disliked, not that he disliked hearing of her fear, only that he desired that she think of him, trust in him, and rely on him to not fear. *Bring my fears to him*, she had learned, in order that he might banish them, for who could fear when he had given his Son for her? The kind of fear then that he detested, she had learned, was fear borne of turning away from him, of directing her concerns to the world rather than to him. He wanted her sharing her issues with him, when she too often had shared her issues only with the world. The world always increased her fears rather than consoled and assuaged them. She had learned that his perfect love drove out all of her fear, that perfect love that his Son had shown the Father in order that the Father might show his love for her. His love had conquered death, when she had learned that death, particularly annihilation without love, rooted all of her fears. Because anticipation of his eternal embrace had replaced her dread of eternal annihilation in a formless abyss, she no longer had reason to fear. All that she need do was to look again to him, to his resurrected Son, and he removed her fear. She could live again, indeed live with courage and generosity in ways that she had never before lived. He was banishing her fear, while replacing it with the promise of his eternal kingdom.

REVELATION

The kingdom was not a fearful place, like her former home had been. The kingdom held surprises, to be sure. In some ways, the kingdom was less predictable than her former home had been. Previously, she could often see both good and bad things coming, welcome things and fearful things arising, sometimes from a long way off. Cause had its effect. Sin led to shame, conflict, and bitter revenge. The world's corruption led to disaster after disaster, one as obvious as the next. The world also held surprises, most of them fearsome things, like horrible illnesses and accidents, and discoveries about others that she would rather not have known. On earth, she hadn't liked surprises. Her outlook had been ominous, never quite ready to let down her guard against the next disaster or threatening disclosure. By contrast, the kingdom's surprises were always welcome surprises. In the kingdom, God was the only cause. God's glory had long ago overwhelmed any sin and corruption, banishing both to earth, from which no new resident brought in any corruption. New residents entered only by the Son's cleansing blood, bringing nothing of their old life with them. Residents thus had no reason to fear the kingdom or anything in the kingdom. Eternal life in sin-free paradise simply eliminated fear as sin's symptom. She no longer had that old sense of foreboding, of just waiting for the next bad thing to happen. The kingdom did not include any of the natural, artificial, or spiritual causes of the dozens of large and small fears that she could once have listed. The darkness had lifted. Everything was now and eternally bright sun.

Sloth

"'Lazy hands make for poverty.'" Proverbs 10:4.

PRAYER

Father, we confess our laziness, idleness, sluggishness, and sloth. You have every right and reason to call us wicked in our indolence. You give us so much good to do, so many with whom to share your word, so many to serve, so many for whom to care. Yet we remain idle, sluggish, and unmoved. While we blame our busy schedules and many cares for ignoring your kingdom work, we are busy only with the distractions and recreations in which we so gladly engage. We leave your good work for another day that never arrives. Our sloth we know to be sin, rank and unjustified turpitude. And we pay the price in poverty. The poverty that we suffer, material in our imaginations though spiritual in the real, is precisely because of our unwillingness to do as you will. You invite us to store up real wealth where wealth actually counts, in your eternal economy, but we instead chase false wealth in a temporary human economy that is both inauthentic and insecure, where we never have enough. Forgive us, Father, even as we turn from our sloth and toward your work with the renewed energy and vigor that comes from pursuing you. We know that sloth is never restful and that we instead find contentment and great gain in you. Give us your heart, the strength and vitality of your glorious Son, and we will no longer be lazy because we will no longer be sinful and corrupt.

ANSWER

Your sloth indeed concerns me, evident most when your thoughts finally turn from your own many desires and ambitious schemes to instead doing my kingdom work. I do not find you slothful when you pursue your worldly ambitions. You are nothing but tirelessly busy at your own ceaseless work. You careen about your days as if they were many in number and with much to gain, pursuing and accumulating material things with an unquenchable desire. Yet when my desires come to your fertile mind, you seem to find many excuses not to pursue them. You feign weariness from our own ambitious labors, when your putative exhaustion looks instead to me more like deliberate sloth. What else am I to call it when you do everything other than my work, pursuing everything other than my desires? You tire yourself with your own labors rather than wearying yourself even once for me. I do not want you exhausted. I do not ask that you give more than you ought, only that you give according to your ability. But so very few do my work with anything approaching the ability that I give them. You are indolent at my work. Your hope thus lies solely in your confession, just as it does for all of your kind. And because you have confessed your sloth, I will remind you again of the completed and perfect work of my Son in whom you wisely trust, while I also send you more of my Spirit. Then you will labor doing my work because my Spirit always awakens you and rids you of your sloth.

TRANSFORMATION

He had of late realized that his ceaseless labors were very likely too much for naught, which was a startling and concerning realization. He had long had the nagging sense that while he wished to labor for God, doing kingdom work, his labors somehow accrued more to his own reputation and benefit than to his Lord's accord. He didn't overtly desire that it be so. He truly wanted to hear the Lord's *well done*. And he did seem to manage consistently to direct his labors for the service, convenience, and benefit of others, perhaps even as much as for his own benefit, which in itself seemed a genuine accomplishment. Yet in doing so, he still had developed an increasing sense that he was not yet doing the Lord's work. In his own view, that troubling sense didn't mean that he must quit his vocation in favor of something that others would immediately recognize as kingdom work, although that possibility certainly existed. Rather, he discerned that in his traditional career and common interactions, he wasn't deliberate enough about what the Lord called him and every other follower to do. That calling was not just to be more holy and righteous, although that would be good too, but to *fish for others* who might join him in following the Lord. He also discovered that he hadn't even equipped himself particularly well to do that fruitful work. And so he turned again to the one person whom he knew could help him most, his beloved Holy Spirit. He daily asked that the Spirit show him his sloth and turn him toward striving, consistent, and effective labor in service of the one great Lord. He knew that the Lord had accomplished an unimaginably compelling and historic salvation mission at the greatest possible cost, with the greatest possible reward for those who embraced it. In sharing that incredibly good news, he no longer had room for sloth.

REVELATION

On one hand, the kingdom didn't seem to require that he work. He no longer, at least, had the sense of earning his keep by the proverbial sweat of his brow. He had entirely lost that old gnawing sense of whether he was doing enough to satisfy others that he was worth his employ. He was no longer living by a sort of daily internal quota of productivity that permitted him rest only when he had accomplished what he thought that others thought he should have done. Unlike his old world, the kingdom certainly didn't seem to be judging how productive or unproductive he was. His labor, such as it was, seemed in no sense tied to his security or pleasure. He certainly had no urgency that he either work or at least appear to others to be working, so as to appear to be worthy of his income and support. None of these liberties surprised him about the kingdom. God satisfied all need and want. He would have been surprised if not. On the other hand, he might previously have thought that he would exhibit no kingdom toil at all, no labor of any sort. Yet to the contrary, if he had cared to take any measure, which he surely did not, then he might have noticed that he actually did more in the kingdom than he had ever previously done. One could not have exactly called it toil or labor because he felt nothing of the sort. While his kingdom activity fully engaged his mind and energies, he still somehow had a full mind for God and abundant excess energy. He never really tired, and his labor, such as it was, never distracted him in the least from the glory of God. Indeed, his labor was entirely for the glory of God. His every action seemed entirely voluntary and with joyful ease for God's honor, even when it entailed strenuous devotion. Kingdom labor was like an energizing dance, not at all a tiring slog.

Ingratitude

"'Has no one but this foreigner returned to give thanks?'" Luke 17:18.

PRAYER

Father, we confess our ingratitude. We fail to acknowledge all or even a small portion of what you do. We pray repeatedly, thinking that you do not answer, when to the contrary you have added a thousandfold in blessings beyond our meager requests. We do not concede your constant gifts and graciousness because our hearts are hard. We turn our vision downward to our circumstance and inward to our desires rather than upward from where you shower down these blessings. In everything, you give us ninety-nine but we want one hundred, while thinking that you have given none. You give us sound function of body and mind, and plenty to live in contentment with you, but we also want beauty, athleticism, or skill. You give us beauty, athleticism, and skill, and we want more of the material things that those attributes might win for us. You give us the material things, and we want the spiritual gifts. You give us the spiritual gifts, and we want the acknowledgment of others that we now possess those gifts in greater proportion than they do. In all these and many similar desires, we consistently fail to thank you, to stop long enough in our insatiable wanting and needing, to see that you have already provided all that we need. Father, we need so badly to thank you, just to admit all with which you have already gifted and graced us. Forgive us, Father, for our ingratitude, even as we learn to see all with which you bless us and to turn back to thank you.

ANSWER

You now begin to see that although I have blessed you so often and richly, you have so frequently failed to turn back from your next desires to acknowledge my former blessing. You do not see me yet as your trusted provider, and so you do not show your gratitude. So in confessing your ingratitude, you are removing a great obstacle between us. I both bless and discipline those whom I choose, intending that my doing so helps you to carry out my purpose, work, and mission for you. When you overlook my blessing and instead see only more of your wants, you frustrate rather than fulfill my will for you. Gratitude is an essential attitude in your accomplishing my mission. Without gratitude, you have little prospect of fulfilling my will. Show me your gratitude, and you will recognize my intentions for you including my love for you. You have no grounds for ingratitude when I gave my Son for you. You have all that you need in my Son, and yet I give you more in order that you might turn to him as your path to all that you need in me. Yes, see my great work for you, and in so doing, also see my loving provision. Enjoy my blessings, but also appreciate them as my doing. I have given you your very breath, the life of my Spirit. Cease in your ingratitude, and take up thanksgiving. And because you have confessed your ingratitude while committing to increasing your thanksgiving, I will show you more of my blessings even as I allow you appropriate challenges while imposing appropriate discipline. You are an unfinished work until you join me. Gratitude becomes you.

TRANSFORMATION

She wasn't grudging in her praise and thanksgiving to God when she thought of him. Her heartfelt thanksgiving was often joyous, profound, and profuse. Her challenge, though, was that she thought of him far too seldom. She knew that she needed to *think* of him more often in order to *thank* him more often. She had heard of various practices like starting each day with thanksgiving prayer or even setting a quiet alarm to remind one to thank God every hour or few hours. Yet she didn't particularly want to make a discipline out of thanksgiving. Her God was not a clock god, not one whom she felt would appreciate that she needed a literal reminder. She would much rather, as she suspected that God would much rather, that her discipline pass quickly through duty into devotion and delight. Of all things, she didn't want her thanksgiving to be forced, formal, or grudging. She wanted her thanksgiving to spring from her heart spontaneously, even if she knew that she also wanted thank him more often. God wanted loving relationship, her thanksgiving flowing from a glad heart. As she thought through her conundrum, she gradually settled not so much on forcing or timing gratitude but removing *ingratitude*. She realized that she grumbled more often than she had thought, far more often than she ought. She didn't need to set any clock to remind her of thanksgiving. Her grumbling became her reminder. Every little self-assessment that she found herself making throughout the day, when previously she might have grumbled, reminded her just how much she owed and loved God. Soon, even on her hard days, indeed especially on her hard days, she found herself thanking God for his endless miracles, even for the refining and reminding hardships.

REVELATION

To her great relief, the kingdom solved another one of the nagging quandaries for which she had formerly felt frequent guilt while feeling powerless to address it. In her former state, she had felt nearly constant ingratitude even while wanting to thank God for everything. She had known intellectually that she owed God everything and that he supplied all. She had somehow, though, gone about life largely grumbling about one thing or another rather than thanking him. God wasn't responsible for the things about which she grumbled. She hadn't meant to outright blame him for anything. She just hadn't found much time or occasion to do so, especially given her grumbling attitude. The kingdom solved that conundrum. With sin and corruption absent, and her own devotion in her transformed state consistently pure, she had no grounds or cause for grumbling. With every kingdom moment a delight, and God so evidently delight's lone and generous source, all that she had to show for her attitude was unrelenting gratitude. She went about every moment with nothing but thanks to God. Appreciation was now her natural and steady state, uninterrupted by anything. She showed her gratitude in several ways, mostly in her constantly bright attitude and demeanor but also in words of gratitude, both silent and spoken, and praise songs, both hummed and sung aloud. She also found herself frolicking at times in euphoric mix of praise and gratitude, an odd marvel that always made her think of King David's delight before the Lord. The kingdom had solved her ingratitude problem, and its resolution was indeed delight.

Pride

"Pride goes before destruction." Proverbs 16:18.

PRAYER

Father, we confess our pride. We confess that we place ourselves above you and others, taking credit for things that you authorize, that others accomplish, and that we failed to do. In arrogance and conceit, we claim special attributes that we do not have while denying those attributes to you and to others who also possess them. Our pride indeed goes before our fall. We have fallen far in our pride, so far as to be estranged from you. Yet while others see and despise our pride, we know that you through the sacrifice and redemptive work of your Son will look past our pride when we repent of it. We here trust in your Son and repent, enabling you to bring us back to you. Help us, Father, to turn from our pride. Help us to see ourselves as we truly are, which is incomplete, broken, and so often less than those around us. Grace us with your Son's humility, Father, in which he credited all to you. Give us that emancipating insight into our fatal insufficiency and concomitant need for you. We have no need to usurp your glory, for glory means nothing to us apart from you. We confess our arrogance, struggle against our superiority, condemn our conceit, and reject our pride. As we do so, draw us back to your eternal kingdom, Father, where all is your glory and where you decide who deserves your acknowledgment. We want your honor, not our own honor. We want to elevate you, not to elevate ourselves, for from high places we know that we will fall. Even though in our pride we may try to think more of ourselves than we ought, we cannot credibly credit ourselves. You hold our only esteem and reward. Accept our prayer in which we confess our arrogance.

ANSWER

You do well to confess your arrogance because none can arrogate my glory. Everything is mine, from which none can appropriate anything other than that which I warrant for them. I have chosen to give honor and glory to my Son who glorified me for the benefit of all of you. Thus your only honor and glory is in your worship of me through my glorified Son. When you take on the image of my Son, I see in you my Son with whom I share my glory. Your pride is your own, and anything that is your own is not mine and thus has no glory. You must give up your pride to have anything that becomes you, anything that attracts me to you and justifies my sharing my honor as I do only with my Son. When you claim your own glory, of which you have none, you accomplish nothing more than to reject me and my Son. Yes, you will find people to honor you, but they will do so only with false lips for the momentary advantage that doing so may garner them. They will turn from you as quickly as their advantage turns, which is as quickly as you lose the power to grant them what they desire. In that way, you are all alike in seeking to fulfill your own desires with your own honor. You will all fall just as far as you lift yourselves up in false and temporary honor. You, though, have confessed your pride. Few of you are willing to so confess because so few of you see your pride in your own actions, only seeing pride in others. Because you have confessed your pride, I will show you more of my glory. As I show you more of my glory, you will lose more of your desire for anything other than my glory. Then you will know what it means to live as I made you to live in the fullness of my Spirit.

TRANSFORMATION

He could see his pride as clearly as he could see his hands when he raised them up in worship to God before him. He knew the moment that he acted out his pride. He even knew that others could see his frequent conceit while also knowing that those others quietly mocked and silently condemned him for it. He knew better than to act in arrogance, knew that doing so was wrong. Yet he did so anyway, like a moth to flame, expecting and even embracing his own destruction. In this question of pride, he knew right from wrong but felt powerless to do right and stop the wrong. In his corrupted state, prideful displays looked like quenching water to him, even though he knew that they satisfied nothing and that he would be just as thirsty for approbation afterward as before. The difference that seemed gradually to have taken hold of him, though, was that he was discovering what did satisfy, what did quench his thirst for glory. He was learning not to try the impossible of soaking glory in but instead to do the possible and appropriate, which was to point all glory to God. He could then turn his striving not to attract praise to himself but to call attention to the glory of God. If, as he knew, he was hopelessly limited and foolish, and his many shortcomings pitifully transparent to everyone, then anything that his efforts accomplished would indeed be to the glory of God. If, as he knew, God could use a donkey to teach a prophet, then maybe he'd just keep plodding onward in his efforts like the donkey and in doing so bring some odd glory to God. Whenever he sensed his pride once again pitifully on display, he thought of the donkey and smiled. Let people see him as a donkey. Just let them see in the pitiful donkey's work the authentic glory of God.

REVELATION

The kingdom addressed pride in a manner that he had not anticipated. He knew that the kingdom would give no place to personal pride. With God's glory on full display, the kingdom could not do so. The kingdom had only one King. Unlike famous figures on earth who at times possessed degrees of honor and glory, sometimes greater and other times less, and always at risk and in flux, God's kingdom glory was always full and complete. And unlike the honor of famous figures on earth, which seemed to depend largely on how well the public regarded them, God's glory was also independent of the praise, honor, or credit of others. Kingdom residents certainly saw, appreciated, and reveled in God's glory, all of which pleased God. Yet their dances and shouts of praise could not add to that glory. Nothing could add to glory that was already infinite and complete. Because the residents' public worship did not add to God's glory, their periodic cessation of worship in favor of quiet praise and reflection did not detract from God's glory in the least. As scripture promised, the kingdom indeed gave evident reward to each according to each's kingdom treasure stored up while still on earth. Yet evident to every resident was that no resident had any need of individual honor, given that each resident's security in God was so complete. Further, no resident had any possibility of honor apart from God. God's radiant glory simply filled the kingdom. Rewards were possible, frequent, and evident, but pride had no place. He found the full kingdom equation complex but entirely satisfactory. He also found it a great relief from the overweening striving that marked and degraded ambitions on earth. The kingdom left no one empty. God's glory filled all.

Impatience

"God's people grew impatient on the way." Numbers 21:4.

PRAYER

Father, we confess our impatience. We admit how we rush ahead of your plans and providence for us without even thinking of you. When in our hurry we do think of you, we think incorrectly that you are not thinking of us. We assume, wrongly, that you are not acting promptly enough for us. Rather than patient and trusting in you, we are faithless and restless, always on the move, particularly when you would have us hold still to see *you* move. Failing to trust in you, rely on you, and wait for you, we act out of our own will rather than discerning and following your will. To justify acting as we wish, we attribute to you an imaginary reluctance to care and provide for us, and to shelter and protect us, knowing that we do so against your covenant, nature, and word. In our impatience, we rationalize pursuit of our own desires, assuming and asserting that you are late, inattentive, and busy with or distracted by other and greater concerns. As the great Father of the glorious Son, your enduring concern and care is for us, your Son-redeemed people. Yet we act impatiently, impulsively, even irritably and impetuously, like children of parents who are the same. Because we know who you are and for whom you care, Father, we should be enduring, trusting, and content. Help us to be so, while forgiving our disquietude, impetuosity, and haste.

ANSWER

You are an impatient person living among impatient and perverse people. You think that in your rushing you accomplish more when in fact without waiting for me you accomplish far less. What you accomplish without me has no value and instead causes much harm.

Why don't you wait for me? You have correctly answered my question when you acknowledge your lack of faith. When you act without me, you do so because you do not believe that I will act, when I always act in the right time for action. To learn to wait for me, you must learn to trust me. You must grow in faith. To grow in faith, you must evaluate your experience because experience alone does not teach. You must listen to my Spirit in order to see how your hasty action does not serve my will. My Spirit will help you interpret your experience until you discern my movement in everything. Then you will pause to see my action. Then you will properly hesitate, look, listen, hear, see, and follow me when you act. I will lead you, not in fruitless haste but in purposeful and fruitful action. And because you have confessed and turned from your haste, I will now help you remain steadfast, close, and connected to me. Your action will bear the fruit that I intend. That fruit will bless you and others, even as it glorifies my Son and me. When I act, good follows. When you act, be sure that you do so with me.

TRANSFORMATION

She, like nearly everyone whom she knew, was impatient, or if not exactly impatient, then at least *restless*. Indeed, she was so restless that her family and friends made frequent polite and humorous note of it, as in *there she goes again*. She wasn't sure of the source of her restlessness, although she sensed that it had increased rather than decreased. She also wasn't sure that her restlessness was a bad thing rather than a good thing, just as her friends and family didn't make it out to be either good or bad. What, after all, was wrong with activity, with vitality, even if it did sometimes leave people and things in its figurative wake? As she scrutinized her increasing urge to be in motion, to be always *on the go*, she slowly began to see a spiritual component to it. She had long considered her motion to have little or nothing to do with her relationship with God, which she treasured above all things. Yet somewhere deep in her spirit she discerned that everything, including this constant-motion thing, had to do with her relationship with God. She began then to question her motion, test her activities, even as she contemplated, planned, and executed them. She didn't exactly slow down, although here and there she felt as if she was pausing, maybe even letting God forge ahead. Then the realization dawned on her. She had not really admitted that God was constantly in motion in her life. Her life had forever been *her* life rather than the life and Spirit of God moving and acting in and through her. She needed to connect her motion with the movement of God because her motion expressed her will, and her will, she knew, needed to be the will of God. Pause, look, listen, and consider, she thought. And then when you see God acting, *move*.

REVELATION

Much to her relief, she found that the kingdom was not a place for impatience. The moment that she arrived, she sensed a sort of deceleration from the former frenetic pace that she had maintained on earth. Gone was the world's sickening quickened pace that had left her constantly exhausted. In its place was a sort of unfolding of events. She felt almost as if she was reeling events in at exactly the pace that they should occur, except that she did not really feel as if she controlled the perfect pace of those events. Indeed, perhaps that sense of not controlling events was just what relieved her of her former exhaustion. Because she was not in control *and knew it*, she had in effect to just relax. Events just developed spontaneously in perfect timing, without either rushing up on her or lagging behind and arriving late, after her attention had passed. She couldn't sense why or how everything came together precisely in its good time, although of course she knew that God was the cause. One moment, she thought that the kingdom had transformed her. The next moment, she felt that the kingdom itself was different. God was plainly so exquisitely in control, his actions so undistorted by the world's sin, that of course everything should happen in symphonic order and timing. He was the great conductor. The constant gorgeous unfolding that his conducting produced entirely satisfied her own sense of timing. The kingdom had made her different, but the kingdom itself was different from the world. God had timed both her and the kingdom to his tempo. Not once did she have the sense of impatience that had haunted her into bursts of frivolous action more often than she had wanted to admit. Her lack of faith and confidence in God, her unwillingness to rely on him to initiate his action, was gone. She now relied entirely on his movement, entirely to her relief. The kingdom resolved the sin of impatience just as it resolved every other sin.

Anger

"Get rid of all bitterness, rage, and anger." Ephesians 4:31.

PRAYER

Father, we confess our bitterness, anger, and rage. Small and large obstacles and annoyances, things that a sensible person would readily overlook, instead irk us. Small things, forgettable and forgivable things, instead make us quarrelsome and contentious even with those whom we ought to most love. Where you command love, we too often exhibit hardhearted hatred and disgust in which we turn others not just from ourselves but from you. Why, Lord, do we seethe, why do we rage? We hold onto too much of ourselves while resisting too much of you. If we had more of your Spirit, the Spirit of your Son, then we might do as he did, forgiving and praying for even those who tortured and crucified him. If your Son could sacrifice himself for us in love, when he could instead have justly raged at and condemned both his tormentors and us, then we certainly need more of his Spirit, more of your Holy Spirit, and far less of ourselves. Yes, others neglect, overlook, offend, and disrespect us, even taking what should be ours to claim for themselves. Why, though, should their doing so anger us, when we equally offend and in any case have no cause or standing to keep such a ledger? The only judgment that matters is yours, Father, and so forgive us for our bitterness, bickering, anger, and contention. Instead make of us the deep, sound, absorbent, resilient, and joyful souls reflective of your eternal Spirit.

ANSWER

Your anger indeed offends not just your fellow followers and those whom you should have joining you in my devotion but also me. How can you be angry at my creatures when you are one of them and they, you included, are all mine? I alone judge my creation. You know from my word that when you judge your fellows in anger, you only bring my judgment on you. How can I forgive you your many transgressions when you do not forgive others whom I also wish to forgive? You conceive of yourself far too narrowly. You do not see that I made you to bear offense just as I myself bore offense when sacrificing my Son for you. You have my Spirit's reservoirs of peace and tranquility available to you for the asking, gifts that would carry you through every hardship and past every pain and insult, if you would only ask for and rely on them. You are weak, but I am strong, and my strength is sufficient for you to endure what others demand of you. They give you cause for offense and anger only in the worldly way out of which I have called and saved you. You are not to emote as the worldly emote because then you are just like them. Hold your emotions for me. Leave the worldly to their affectations, and dwell instead in my kingdom where rancor, artifice, and pretension have no place. Love, peace, and patience mark my kingdom, not the seething sin of your broken and corrupt region. And because you have confessed and turned from your anger, I respond once again with generous mercy and ample grace, drawing you into my kingdom where all is indeed peace.

TRANSFORMATION

She didn't like strife, even though she knew that she occasionally caused it, just as she seemed often to receive it. She knew of others who lived and breathed strife to the point that it fed them. She steered clear of those persons, knowing that they fed only on death. Yet even among the better balanced, she saw quickness to anger, swiftness to offense, so much that it should have surprised her if she hadn't also detected that simmering tendency in herself. Rarely, though, she met a person who seemed to absorb offense effortlessly as if they simply soaked it in and dissipated it as quickly as it attacked. Or maybe they rose above it or were already on a different plain. She could see in them that they lived by different rules in a different economy, where one gained nothing for giving back as much or more grief as one got. Their economy seemed instead to depend on a different kind of exchange, one in which the transaction wasn't so much between persons as between the person and God. And she knew that God had long ago confirmed the ledger of offenses as all on one side, his side, leaving humankind without any possible quarrel to pick with God who instead had every quarrel to pick with humankind. He, though, had foregone and forgiven all quarrel. In God's ledger, she found peace whenever she sensed offense, whenever her anger wanted to rise. She would then look quickly away from the offender to God, so that her anger had no cause, and she saw only God's endless mercy and utter redemption for her own grand offense.

REVELATION

The kingdom's remarkable relief from all manner of earthly corruption, burden, and complication, continued to show her the broad dimensions of her former sin. The kingdom of course had no place for anger. She had always known how debilitating both being angry and receiving another's anger could be. Until her kingdom residence, though, she hadn't realized just how offensive worldly anger must have been to God. In their incorruptible state, the kingdom's residents gave no cause to one another for righteous anger. Offense of that kind just did not occur. Jesus had cleansed all entrants of sin. With all in full holiness, no one sinned against another, giving righteous anger no place. And with all in full holiness, unrighteous anger, misdirected and unfair anger, also had no foothold for its mischief. The kingdom's full supply let none compete and none go wanting, removing all manner of potential offense. That God's glory suffused the place further left no room for annoyance or irritation. If any had arisen, which none could, then the glory of the place would instantly have extinguished it. Darkness cannot fall where everything is light. No shadow of exasperation or aggravation was possible, meaning that anger could never take root. The biggest reason, though, that she sensed for the kingdom's absent anger was that God held all kingdom authority. Anger, she knew, presumed judgment. In the kingdom, no one judged another, and thus no one had cause for anger. She realized that her worldly anger, and the anger that others had held for her, had been playing god over others. One didn't play god in the kingdom.

Judgment

"Do not judge, or you too will be judged." Matthew 7:1.

PRAYER

Father, we confess that we judge others when you say not to judge. We confess that we judge others harshly while failing to see our own faults and judge ourselves accordingly. In doing so, we only condemn ourselves before you. You gave your own Son in order that you might judge only him and not us. You redeemed us with your judgment requiring the greatest possible price of his blood. You nonetheless properly hold that you will still judge us if after receiving your mercy we continue to judge others. And yet judge others is exactly what we do. We always judging others short of the glory that you have bestowed on them in the image of your redeemer Son. How could we so affront you? Our only hope is in our confession of our critical spirit and our commitment to turn away from it. We must abjure ourselves of judgment's practice even if we cannot alone cleanse ourselves of its stain. You take this affront, too, under the cleansing blood of your sacrificed Son. You resurrect and restore us to you through your Son's own resurrection. You are the merciful Lord, the one who judges but does not judge. You are the one who judged your own Son that you would not judge us who embrace, honor, and cherish him. Father, forgive us for our critical and judging spirit. Help us not to judge and condemn anyone lest you judge and condemn us.

ANSWER

Having given my only Son in judgment of all, I indeed judge nothing of you who seek his sheltering blood. How could I look past my Son's own glorious sacrifice, that which absolved and hid all wrong? I see only his exquisite obedience in his give-it-all love. My Son died for you that I would not judge you and that you would have no cause to judge. Judgment is indeed mine alone, and I have chosen not to judge beyond having accepted my Son's own life in judgment's eternal satisfaction. Word comes in confession to me that you have nonetheless judged, but with your confession that wrong, too, is under the blood of my Son. You have joined my confessing church, the fellowship of those who see and turn from their sin. I accept your commitment not to judge, knowing that you will still judge again but expecting that you will then recommit in confession all over again. You know your sin nature, that which died with my Son. Although you still see and sense it, your critical spirit has no control over your destiny, which is now instead mine. I will resurrect you without your fatal critical spirit so that you will have eternal life with me. Judging is just your past. Forgiveness is for your future. Because you have confessed your judgmental spirit, I will not judge you but instead leave all judgment under the purifying blood of my Son. You will join me in eternity.

TRANSFORMATION

He had no need to judge anyone and for the most part didn't. He tried to keep to himself so that no one could give him any cause. Better, he felt, to keep his eyes fixed on Jesus because he sensed the desire to judge the moment he fixed his eyes on others. He recognized that the moment his mind turned to others, his first inclination was in judgment, as if he had some right, claim, or stake to live *their* lives. He knew that judgment was the oddest way to think of others because judgment did neither them nor him any good. Judgment led quickly to disrespect and disdain, to disregard and division. He also knew judgment's eternal consequences, that he needed no judgment, disrespect, or disdain from God. So each time he thought of another and began to sense his judging spirit in operation, he would instead force himself to think good of them, to count their strengths and successes rather than their failures and flaws. When he came to that point, he found it easy to think of such good things. Everyone he knew had many things to recommend them, even if their flaws were equally evident. He found himself happier, more willing to speak kindnesses and encouragement, when he was thinking good of others. He could see in such good thoughts and words a ministry of sorts. Encouraging words healed, where judgment wounded and offended. In his confession and rejection of his own judgmental mind, God was indeed blessing him with both a salving and saving ministry.

REVELATION

The kingdom indeed resolved the question of judgment immediately, fully, and finally. He had come soon to realize that he took no note of the conditions of others and of things in the kingdom. In retrospect, he realized that on earth, he had naturally evaluated, judged, and determined almost constantly. Maybe judging had been the nature of the place, or maybe judging was his own corrupt character. He had just felt then, in his former place, that he had better be making determinations of all kinds of things, including the character and actions of people. He hadn't always communicated his judgments, although sometimes he had. He had known God's admonition not to judge others, but he just hadn't managed not to do so and couldn't really see how to avoid judging. The kingdom, though, not only made judging unnecessary, given the holy state of every resident. He could see immediately that other residents gave him no fair grounds to judge, just as the kingdom's paradise gave him no conditions to evaluate negatively. The kingdom also made judging a practical impossibility. God, whom every resident knew held all authority, was present. While on earth, God had delegated authority to others even in their corruption, in the kingdom God had not delegated authority. With God present and holding all authority, no resident had any standing on which to judge. To judge another would have been to contradict God in his presence, which his replete authority simply did not permit. Every resident's knee had already bowed, and gladly, not stubbornly. No resident had any desire to usurp any part of God's throne, when judging would have been exactly that kind of usurping. The world had held all manner of little persons playing god, judging others. The kingdom held but one God. The still-new resident felt enormous relief at not having any cause or standing to evaluate, determine, and judge.

Secrecy

"Cursed is anyone who sets up an idol in secret." Deuteronomy 27:15.

PRAYER

Father, we confess that we pursue secret ways other than your ways. We ignore or forget that you know all that we think and see all that we do. In secrecy we harbor thoughts that you abhor, in secrecy we speak slander that you condemn, and in secrecy we commit acts that you detest. We arrogantly presume ourselves safe from your judgment when we successfully hide from others what we think and do, as if what others think of us is how you judge us. In reality, though, we seldom successfully hide our corruption from others, while we never successfully hide our sin from you. Still somehow, even while knowing your omniscience, we act as if you are deaf, blind, and dumb, as if you would not hear, see, and speak of our wrongs. We secretly think and speak hatred for those whom you love. We judge others where you would forgive them. We withhold from others to whom you would generously give. In doing so, we trust that you are looking the other way, as if you concern yourself with us only when we behave. Indeed, you do look the other way but in disgust for our secret thoughts and actions rather than in ignorance of what we think and do. Help us turn from our secret ways, Father. Help us live lives of purity both outside where others see us and inside where you see. Give us more of your Holy Spirit and less of our own spirits in which we try to conceal our wrongs as we commit them clandestinely. Let your light bring all corruption into the open where we must turn from it and have you heal us. Forgive us, Father, for our secret ways.

ANSWER

You do nothing in secret that I do not know. Your hidden ways are as obvious to me as what you do in public. Your heart I see, and your mind I know. You harbor nothing from me, before whom all is exposed. Secrecy is impossible before the omniscient. If you would only live as if I know all, which I do, then you would prosper where you currently fail.

Your exposed heart would heal. Your corrupt mind would recover pure thoughts, and you would live a righteous life accordingly. Live openly before me. Let my holy standard, the conscience that I alone impose, keep you pure. No longer live by your secret thoughts. Live transparently and exposed. As my word says, you are wretched, pitiful, poor, blind, and naked. Everyone can see you as you are rather than as you wish to be. So you may as well turn your wishing toward me. Let my light, my exposure, change your innermost thoughts. Let my scrutiny remove from you more of your sodden dross. Then you will find your steps lighter and truer because you have yoked yourself to me. You will have let my mind guide you, my words direct your paths. You will no longer be living the secret life that you currently live as sin's slave but instead a life of liberty, slave only to me, when my will is to set all free. Turn yourself loose of your secret ways, not by hiding them further but by confession and correction under my inspection. Know that I watch and see. And because you have confessed your secrecy, I will relieve you of its burden, bring you into the light, and purify you of its stain, free in my mercy and buoyed by my grace, with liberty at last.

TRANSFORMATION

She didn't feel particularly secretive, not like some others seemed to be. She wanted to think, rather, that she was an open book. Yet as she thought about her own thoughts, she realized that they were just as secretive as anyone else's thoughts. Secrecy was natural to her human condition. No one could read her thoughts, and she *knew* that no one could read her thoughts, a knowledge that she then recognized was dangerous. Transparency was what she liked about younger children. They didn't screen their thoughts. Their mouths said just what they were thinking, which at least kept them honest about their intentions, even if their honesty didn't always work well for them. Better, perhaps, that they soon learn to hide their thoughts. Yet that hiding of one's thoughts was exactly the problem, she knew, because it allowed all manner of deviousness. One could then be corrupt inside but put on a show outside, which was what Jesus condemned. So, she reasoned, the strategy and principle must be to think pure thoughts, as if Jesus knew her thoughts, which he plainly did. Her heart hid no intentions from its creator. She could then live like a little child, which she knew perfectly well that Jesus also admonished. In that sense, living with integrity, outside matching in, was actually a childlike condition, she concluded. Jesus wasn't so concerned with a child's silliness and lack of experience or reason because to Jesus all are foolish and lacking in reason. Jesus was instead concerned that she should have a pure heart. She was going to wear her heart on her sleeve, but her heart was going to be Jesus's pure heart.

REVELATION

The kingdom did not know secrecy. She found in the kingdom no such need nor cause. God of course was omniscient, one from whom no kingdom resident could in the least hide. No resident tried. After all, with all residents washed in Jesus's blood and held without stain, none had anything to hide. Yet kingdom life freed her from more than fear of God's discovery. She also found no need to hide from other residents. The transparency and confidence of kingdom life taught her that life in the world had been one long deceit, one long charade and fraud. Of course, worldly beings were naturally corrupt, always ready to conceal and hide. But moreover, earthly life did not permit full disclosure. The world was so lacking in mercy and grace that on full disclosure, none would have survived. Deceit in the sense of putting on airs to make one look better than one was, was everywhere, so much so that its absence would have been alarming. In the kingdom, everyone represented themselves exactly as they were both because no resident had sin to conceal and because no resident had any fear of adverse judgment. God had already washed and pardoned all residents. With God holding all authority to judge and thus having forgiven, no resident could judge another. Every resident stood perfectly free to be who they were. None had any need for secrets. Indeed, the kingdom was so thoroughly holy and thus authentic in every respect, that everyone and everything appeared exactly as he, she, or it was. She felt another great relief from another previously consternating worldly burden. Nothing had solved her worldly need for secrecy until she reached the kingdom.

Deceit

"Rid yourselves of all deceit." 1 Peter 2:1.

PRAYER

Father, we confess our deceit and deception. We twist and exaggerate truth, we subtly mislead, and we outright lie. We do so always to gain credit, property, or other interest that is not ours but instead belongs to you or others. We are born liars but, by your mercy, reborn to know and speak your truth. We are native dissemblers whom you remade to reveal only the authentic and real. Why would you, the wholly righteous God, have anything to do with us, we whom the world knows as much for our trickery and cons as for any semblance of righteousness? Your mercy remains our greatest mystery, answered only in that we carry your image and love your Son. You saved us, cheaters and swindlers whose only merit was to hide in the blood of your Son, simply to show how much you loved your Son. Through your love for your Son, you loved us, your pitiful and pathetic creature frauds. Your word is the only truth that we know. The one thing that we speak honestly, without a trickster's distortion, is your word, the word of God. Let no one know us for anything other than that we follow you, oh great Father. If they knew us for any other reputation than our pursuit of your word, then they should not trust us. Trust us only for knowing and pursuing you. We do not give the world our own righteousness, of which we certainly have none. Instead, we show the world you, the Holy One, whose word is true. Do not let us continue to speak lies and deceit, oh Father, but let us speak your truth. For what is true, indeed *who* is true, other than you?

Answer

I despise dissembling because I am truth. Your lies deny not just fact and reality but also deny me. They reject that I am, turning you and others away from your creator toward your own imaginings that will do nothing for you. To lie is to deny that I exist and will hold all accountable. You know truth only when you know me. Without me, all is distortion. With me, all is truth. Your false assertions do not measure me because I am the creator and arbiter of all that is true. Your schemes, scams, and swindles are your own creation, every one of them evidence of your hopeless condition without me. Everything that you do apart from me is worse than worthless, full of destruction. You must learn to stay closer to me, to profess me rather than to propagate your godless lies. When you stay close to me, speaking my word rather than your own, you reveal truth. My thoughts and words cleanse you of your foul deceit. Your measures become accurate and your words worthy of confidence, ready for others to trust. Speak of me as I am, and you will speak truth. You will convey value to your hearers rather than sell them worthless myths and harmful lies. Your reputation will grow with your honesty, and your trade will then spread instead of diminish. With your own false words, you will garner nothing and soon die. With my true word, you will store up riches and live forever. Because you have confessed and turned from your deceit, I will send my Spirit to remind you of more of my word so that your mouth will bless others. In blessing others with my true word, you will earn your just reward.

TRANSFORMATION

God's Spirit had given him a conscience, and that conscience had shown him his lies. He at first had thought that they were small or even innocent deceits. He had gradually learned that they were neither small nor innocent. No one lies about the inconsequential. Every lie has its aim, and that aim is universally to reward its perpetrator. The little lie leads to the big lie until all is deceit and nothing trustworthy. He thanked God for the Spirit's showing him just how untrustworthy were his words. His growing conscience, a rich blessing of the Spirit, had then shown him actions that were deceitful, habits that he needed to abandon or correct. He hadn't at first thought those habits harmful because everyone seemed to do them. Yet he soon realized just how harmful they were. Their prevalence, making them seem so innocuous, only increased their ready acceptance and thus magnified their harm. As the Spirit led him forward, he expected to find in himself fewer and fewer flaws. Instead, his every advance in holiness revealed to him ever greater deceit. He eventually concluded that he would not find holiness within him but only in God. He was fatally corrupt, but the Spirit of God was now living more freely within him, making for him a new self in which all was God and thus all was holiness. Try as he might, he could not reform his old self into something better. Instead, he could only gradually abandon his old self as the Spirit showed him. Thank God that he had a new self, one in whom he found no deceit. He had only to learn to stop clinging to the old self.

REVELATION

Hand in hand with banishing secrecy, the kingdom also banished deceit. In his former life, he hadn't felt particularly deceitful. Certainly, schemes, scams, swindles, and frauds had been no part of his intentions. Yet kingdom life showed him an entirely new dimension of integrity, one that made his former life look exactly like a scheme, scam, or swindle. His kingdom life was just so pure. Every intention led to action consistent with the intention. When he thought of something, he simply carried it out just as he had intended. His consistency of thought to action made kingdom life so much simpler than his former life. He wasn't constantly intending one thing but accomplishing another and then having to deal with the inconsistency between the two, usually (in his former life) by some form of cover up. In kingdom life, the outcomes were as he wished, and so he had no need for exaggerating, diminishing, or otherwise construing intent to more or less match outcome. Moreover, his intentions were pure. He had none of that old sense of the old man desiring things that his heart and mind didn't exactly approve, and his heart and mind thus putting new twists to old intentions. Every part of his new self aligned, heart to mind and intentions. His intentions and their following actions and outcomes were also good. He had a clarity of purpose that his former self had lacked. The difference, of course, was that he could see clearly the will of God. He never had a sense of going it alone. God's desire was always evident before him, making his intentions and actions as easy as gladly submitting to that which God had planned. He no longer had any deceit in him because he held tight to the guiding hand of God.

Carnality

"The world stirs lust of the eyes and flesh." 1 John 2:16.

PRAYER

Father, we confess our lust of eye and flesh. In our carnal nature, we covet that which is not ours, should not be ours, and would do us no good if it were ours. In our broken natural condition, we want things that you forbid and that we know would not be good for us. We desire those forbidden and destructive things as if bent within our own flesh toward them, that unhealthy desire itself a natural force emanating from within us. We also desire those forbidden and destructive things when tempted by the sight of them, drawn to them from outside of us. Desire and temptation thus join forces from inside and outside of us, stirring our lust into a continual vortex down which we feel we must slide, when our own desire, indeed our own selfish will, is that which pulls us. Your Spirit turns us from these forbidden and destructive desires, away from ourselves and toward your Son. You crucified our carnality so that we may live in the holiness of your Son. In your Son, we have new life that no longer pursues our own desires but instead desires and pursues greater things in you. While desire's destructive old vortex continues in our old life, pulling the old person down, we no longer live our old life but instead have adopted your new life, which is life in your Son. Forgive us for our lustful desires, Father, while we turn resolutely and joyfully to new life in your Son. We confess that desire still haunts us but only as memorial to all that your Son has won.

ANSWER

Your carnal desires condemned and consumed you until I sent you my Son. You had no remedy or relief, no way to escape your insatiable urges until I gave you my Son as righteous way. My Son took your corruption to the cross, where it suffered its rightful shameful death. It no longer has any power over you because you have the power, protection, and purity of my Son. You no longer carry the stain of your satisfied urges. All that my Son has touched with his absolution is holy, all is pure. Your guilt no longer guides you, your shame no longer holds you down. My Spirit attends you and my angels guard you. You are mine, free from all that enslaved you. You need only follow my Son, love my Son, heed my Spirit. I am your savior God. I do not condemn you. Your lusting no longer binds you when you live in the liberty of my love, the righteous path of my Son. You have confessed your old nature while adopting the new, taking on the life and image of my holy Son. Your new self lives free of old ways, walking in my kingdom where all is life and death has no grasp. Because you give up the old flesh for the new Spirit, confessing your past while reaching for your future, I will guard you from the old desires while increasing your new desire for me. You will walk confidently in my kingdom, no longer burdened by your past, but emboldened and refreshed by your future.

TRANSFORMATION

He could look back, way back, and see that God had changed him. He still had the sense of his old self right there with him, that old nature that just desired, it almost didn't matter what. Yet that old nature didn't have the same control over him that it once did. He could sense clearly that he also had a new nature, new but also maturing, growing stronger and clearer. That new nature drew from God's word and Spirit. It didn't follow the old urges. He could clearly sense the two natures within him, even though he committed only to the new one. The old nature didn't really compete with the new nature as much as try to distract him from it. Any competition seemed long ago to have resolved in favor of the new and against the old. Their relationship, between old and new, wasn't a question of greater right, purpose, or power, for the old nature had nothing on the new. They were not simply opposites but enemies in a war that the new had undoubtedly won. Indeed, he relied on the new nature's victory whenever he felt the distraction of the old. He would look again to the cross, where he saw the old, and then to the resurrection, where he saw the new. The more that he looked to the cross over the years, the more that the new self stood out, and the less that the old self served to distract him. The old self was still right there, but he didn't hear it so often. When he did hear it, he didn't heed it, instead turning again to the resurrection where all he saw was the new.

REVELATION

His kingdom body was definitely different from his former abode or, as he felt then and how it may well have been, his former prison. He knew that his body was formerly God's temple and still now remained so, whether on earth or in heaven. He no longer had, though, the sense that his body was working against God's Spirit. Then, his spirit had been willing but his flesh obviously weak. Nearly every time that his spirit had soared after the desires of God, his body had protested, fallen behind, and collapsed. When his spirit had rested, his body had whined, entreated, and nagged. He had then the sense that he didn't much control his body, at least not its desires and intentions. His mind would say one thing but his body another. His will wanted to pursue God, but his body wanted to pursue itself. His body had always wanted things that it did not have and should not have. His body had also always wanted more of whatever it *did* have, even more than was good for it. In the kingdom, though, his resurrected body had no desire independent of that which his spirit pursued. Indeed, kingdom life was almost as if his body's incorruptible health and vitality led his spirit on to greater good things. Far from lagging behind, his body leapt ahead even when his mind might have questioned whether his body could accomplish the challenge that God had so graciously put before him. He supposed that his resurrected body was like that of a perpetual youth, although his earthly youth hadn't truly offered anything like his current constant supply of good vitality. In the kingdom, every molecule seemed to dance right along with the desires of God. His body had no desultory mind or laggard spirit of its own. God had conformed and trained his body to the mind and life of the Spirit. His prison had opened, and he had flown.

Superiority

"Do not consider yourself to be superior." Romans 11:18.

PRAYER

Father, we confess our superiority. We confess that we place ourselves above you and others to whom we are in no sense superior. We strive vainly to represent ourselves as greater not just than we actually are, which would in itself be a prideful offense, but greater than others, which compounds our offense. Indeed, we foolishly consider ourselves better than others whom you hold as your own family members, your own children, who are brothers and sisters of your Son. How could we be so thoughtless as to consider those whom your Son redeems to be anything other than our full equal? Do we have a greater redemption? Do we sit at your right hand while others sit at your feet? Dear Father, help us to turn from superior conceits in which we look down on those whom you have raised up, while we hold ourselves high when you would have us humble. You know our lofty vanities, which to you are nothing but selfish evils and depravities. We confess these spiritual crimes. We embrace your Son's humility in order that you see past our decadences. Do not look on us in the false light in which we hold ourselves but rather look on us in the true light of your Son. We are not our past but our future, in image uniquely made like your own beloved Son.

ANSWER

Your conceits would amuse me if they were not so deadly. When you hold yourself above others who are at least your equal, you remove yourself from the shelter of my Son. No one who lifts one's self above others can bear the image of my Son who placed himself below all in order to serve all. You should bear the burdens of others as my Son did and then let my Son lift you up. You know that I lift the humble while lowering the arrogant. Humility attracts me to you, while your arrogance repels all. When you act in superiority, you pretend no need of me. When you are humble, you call on my glory and strength. Your superiority pushes me far from you, where you would perish without me. Your humility fills you with my Spirit, giving you eternal life. You have no need for arrogance, which can neither feed nor fill nor save you.

You have no power to lift yourself up, for from whom or what would you lift? I am the only rock and salvation. I am the only one who can raise anyone up. I lifted my Son in order that he would glorify me. My Son lifted you out of the mire of your arrogance, setting you on your feet. Because that mire is your natural home, you have no ground on which to raise yourself above any others, just as they have no ground to raise themselves above you. My Son is your only ground, the rock on whom you stand before me. These things your confession admits. And so because you have confessed the rule of my Son while admitting your prior arrogance, I see you now as humble once again and worthy to see my glory. When you see my glory, you will know why I cannot countenance arrogance.

TRANSFORMATION

She detested arrogance in others, even as she hated to see it in herself. The problem was being able to see it in herself as much as she could detect it in others. She supposed that was arrogance's nature, that it only looked so to others and not to one's self. She knew that everyone needed a lift while too few got it. The world was short of honor, credit, and praise, and long on the desire for them. She saw in just about everyone the self-protective tendency toward holding one's self in higher esteem to satisfy what others did not honor. The few who did not seek their own honor seemed somehow to have either avoided or satisfied the need. They just seemed more secure than others, less in need of feeling full of themselves, more ready to empty themselves of any concern for themselves. They had let themselves go somehow, as if they didn't need the mooring in rank that others needed. She wanted to be equally free from rank, equally without need of superiority over anyone. She knew that her hope for freedom from that striving self-promotion was in Jesus's accomplishment, the victory that he shared with so many so generously. The only thing that she needed for any sense of notice was that she shared his victory. Let her sole honor be his glorious accomplishment, she figured. If anyone wanted to credit her with anything, then let them credit her with *that*. And if no one wanted to give her any credit, then she had plenty already in eternal life. She had the one critical credit, the eternal life of the Son, from the only one, the glorious Father, who ultimately mattered.

REVELATION

She was entirely relieved that the kingdom had one utterly clear superior who was God. The kingdom eliminated any question over who among the many residents had the greater rank. If rank there had been, which for her was a little hard to tell, then every resident was perfectly in agreement and conformity with that rank, which was exactly why she found rank hard to tell. While she identified elders, and elders played special roles, every resident gave instant due to those elders, whom God had clearly ordained. Why would one not do so, she thought? She then remembered that in her former life she might have questioned whom God had elevated or not elevated, especially because everyone, her included, had seemed to have been elevating themselves. On earth, self-promotion had been the norm, giving way to all kinds of competition, dissension, and confusion, while in the kingdom, God ordained whom he wished. None competed, none dissented, and none were confused. On earth, the only solace to chafing under rank was that promotion usually brought with it such hardship that she could be glad that she had not attained the next rank. In the kingdom, none chafed because God had ordered. Everyone had exactly that rank most befitting them. She, for one, felt exactly acquitted for that responsibility which God gave her. Even the elders didn't seem so much superior in rank as specially fitted for the special service that God had them supply. Each, in other words, served according to their unique abilities. God knew her abilities and had given her precisely the proper rank. She felt neither superior nor inferior, only uniquely equipped for those special ordinances that God had given her to execute. She had her ordained role, just as did every other resident. The kingdom eliminated pride, superiority, and conceit.

Idolatry

"You have spent enough time choosing the idolatry of pagans." 1 Peter 4:3.

PRAYER

Father, we confess our idolatry. We confess that we choose other things over you, when you alone are life, and anything else over you is not life but death. We choose ahead of you both good things and bad things, and in choosing the good things ahead of you make of them bad things. We worship you but then worship liberty, love, care, or comfort above you, and in so doing we lose the heart of liberty, love, care, and comfort, which is you. We exalt you but only as long as we have other things with you, whether health or provision or security, when to exalt you truly we must do so unconditionally. We should exalt you without these other things on which our exaltation sadly depends. We want you if we get honor or influence or other things with you, which means that we idolize those things ahead of you. Why is our worship conditional, Father, when you hold all good things and are alone all good? Because we have so many idols, so many things that we value above you, when you alone hold all value, we waste our time on activities and pursuits that take us from you and make us enemies to you. We think ourselves pure but instead carry the stain of idolatry. Father, help us to see that stain, and confess and set aside our vain pursuits, in order that your Son's sacrifice and redemption can complete their work in us. Restore us to you, as we declare of you no equal.

ANSWER

You are right that I have no equal. How can creation call itself equal to creator? Because all issues from me, all is beneath me, all beholden to me, and all mine to do with as I wish. No one equals me because all are subject to me. When I say come, all come, and when I say go, all go. The things that you identify and name are indeed mine to grant or deny and thus less than me. Your devotion should indeed be to me and not to the things that I grant or deny. Your desiring above me that which I grant frustrates my purpose in giving them to you. Why would I give you gifts when you desire the gifts above me? The giver gives to honor the recipient's love of the giver, not of the gifts. I withhold gifts from those who value the gifts above me. Think less of the gifts and more of me, I whom am your giver, and see if I don't shower ever more gifts on you for worshiping me. Your devotion to anything other than me leads you only to death. Your devotion to me leads you into my kingdom where you have eternal life. You devoted your life to me when you accepted my sacrifice of my Son as satisfaction of my judgment on your life. You cannot devote your life to me while treating the things that I create as greater than me. You cannot hold idols above me and still have me. Have no obsessions other than your passion for me. Dedicate yourself to me and only me. And because you have repented of your pursuit of idols, I will reward your devotion to me with greater passion for me. Your passion for me will flower into an earnest love.

TRANSFORMATION

He took many years to appreciate how many and varied his idols could be. Hardly a day passed that didn't lead him to discover another one. When he had first learned of idols, studying God's commands, he had associated them with objects. He at first thought of idols as ancient things that people had worshiped. He gradually came to see that idols could include modern things that people treated with equal devotion, like jewelry, sculpture, literature, music, or art, or even utilitarian objects like homes and cars. People certainly devoted their attention and resources to these things, to the exclusion of other things to which God may well have preferred their attention. People ignored all manner of responsibilities and opportunities for family, friends, service, and care, in favor of these objects. Yet he further realized that devotion could accrue to subjects just as much as objects, like one's rank or reputation, or one's pain or pleasure, or one's life or legacy. He sensed that God accepted that people would attend to many things in the course of a life. Indeed, God had created all things, many of them even for persons' simple pleasure. But he knew, too, that God expected and deserved devotion above all things. So on every day that showed him a new idol, he would set the idol firmly aside, returning his devotion to God. He had no use for idols when he had God's full embrace, in Christ's passion.

REVELATION

Much to his relief, he found that the kingdom held no idols. He hadn't so readily noticed the great number of idols on earth. He had lived among those idols so long that they just seemed not to be idols but instead simply a part of life. Those things definitely wanted his attention, though. Indeed, once in the kingdom, he realized more clearly that everything on earth seemed to want his attention. By contrast, the kingdom somehow directed all attention to God. That God-directedness was in fact the kingdom's most obvious feature. Whereas on earth, everything had drawn his attention from God, in the kingdom everything pointed his attention to God. As with other kingdom experiences, he wasn't sure whether this God-directed experience was an external feature of the kingdom or an internal feature of his own. Probably, it was both external and internal. His incorruptible body was new, and so was the kingdom. His mind, soul, and spirit were all God-directed. Yet the kingdom's signs and symbols, every physical and environmental feature, all also pointed to God. He found no competition for his attention. The effect on him of this God-directed kingdom attribute was likely more extraordinary than the sum of all of his other kingdom experiences. Indeed, he believed after some reflection that all other kingdom attributes were merely corollary to this one primary one. Why, he thought, hadn't he been more attentive on earth to direct his full attention to such a glorious God? No matter, he concluded. That the kingdom was utterly free of idolatrous influences was enormous relief.

3
Thanksgiving

"With thanksgiving, present your requests to God." Philippians 4:6.

Having first adored you, Father, and then confessed our need of you, we also have you to thank and appreciate, only you. As creator and redeemer, you both supply and save. You give life, and then you give hope. We thank and applaud you for both. Without you, we would have no life, while without hope we would have no reason to live. If you had only created us, made us conscious beings, and yet not introduced yourself to us, then we would be without hope and thus living only as the lost. Our lives would be brutish and short, hard and taut, without knowing you as our creator and without access to your kingdom, into which your Son invites us. Without you, we would have no reason to live other than for the momentary satisfaction of our senses, which all eventually recognize is only animal-like, not human life at all. And so we thank and appreciate you not simply for life, which without you would be more like a prison than paradise, but also for you. We thank you for giving us your Son and then your Holy Spirit, and through them giving us you. We are grateful, appreciative, indebted, glad, and gratified in you, Father. We could thank you without end for all who you are and all that you do. Hear our prayers of thanksgiving.

Relationship

"Come near to God and he will come near to you." James 4:8.

PRAYER

We thank you, Father, for relationship with you through your Son. We thank you for the relationship that you maintain with us through your Holy Spirit as comforter and guide, as your divine presence and our friend. Without you, we are nothing more than lost travelers in a foreign and frightening land, on our way to nowhere without companion or purpose, and with precious little time to spare. With you, we have everything for our joyful voyage, on our way to your kingdom to rejoice and glory in you eternally. We have done nothing to earn this relationship with you, dear Father, but instead owe this saving grace entirely to you. You came to us when we did not come to you. You initiated and invited when we had turned away. You extended mercy when all that we deserved was eternal punishment in banishment from you. You brought us back to you through the most astonishing act of sacrifice that humanity will ever know. You did these astounding things for us, Father, because you define yourself as love, and you will never deny yourself. By not turning your back on us, and instead opening your arms so agonizingly wide, you proved yourself to us as the one loving creator God. We thank you, Father, for your willingness to countenance us as our creator, then to forgive us, and in doing so even to walk and talk, eat and drink with us. We thank you for relationship with you.

ANSWER

You know me because I choose for you to know. I desire relationship with my creation. I chose that you of all my creation would be my image. I then took your form as you took mine. I revealed myself in my Son with whom you ate and drank, and whom you knew like a brother. These things I did that you would have relationship with me, and I would have glory from you. All creation honors me, but you alone choose so to do. You have will as I have will. I gave you knowledge and choice in order that you would relate to me, even though only some of you now do. Others abandon me, turn from me, and forget me, or claim to have never known me, even that I do not exist. They do not accept that I made them for relationship with me. They pretend themselves to be uncreated, in order that they not account to me, their creator. Yet they who reject relationship, believing that they are better without me, will perish. You, though, will not perish because you relate to me as only one can, through the love of my Son. You have endeared yourself to him, treating him like the brother and King that he is. You relate to me as you should, both subject to me and intimate with me. I am the God whom you can know. No other is like me. And because you have thanked me for relationship without asking anything of me, I will give you more intimacy with my Son. My Spirit will reveal more of my Son to you, in order that you may dwell with me forever.

TRANSFORMATION

He had felt so alone before he had come to know God. He had always known *of* God but not *known* God. God was a distant deity, not much more than a concept or construct. He had also always known of Jesus, even of Jesus's deity. He had just not yet recognized enough of what God in Christ, the resurrected Christ, meant in relationship terms. God was no distant deity, particularly after having sent his Holy Spirit following Christ's ascension. In his Holy Spirit dimension, the triune God was instead a close, living, breathing, interacting companion, albeit a King-of-kings companion. That daily realization, that God had lived among people and sent his Spirit to commune with people, gradually lessened his sense of being alone. Nearly more than anything else, that one realization was what lifted his veil of loneliness. God wasn't merely a got-it-all-started creator, nor merely a rule maker and judge. God didn't count his every hair and hear his every thought simply as an accountant or psychologist. God could also be his companion. He could converse with God, laugh with God, love with God. He wasn't alone at all. He had just been imagining.

REVELATION

To his unending gratitude, the kingdom gave every resident instant and constant relationship with God. He hadn't realized just how lonely he had been, even though his loneliness was earth's illusion rather than the Spirit's comforting reality. Or maybe, rather than not realizing how lonely he had been, he had instead never realized how rewarding relationship could be. His former life had only had hints of that relationship, foretastes of the sweetness that comes with deeply loving proximity. The kingdom showed him what relationship with the one great loving God really meant. He was no longer trapped as if in a cage, held apart from all others, even if, again, that cage was more illusion than reality. In the kingdom, God had somehow opened his soul so that God's Spirit could flow constantly and reassuringly both in and out. In his corrupted earthly state, he had never let the Spirit have such free reign of him. He had held tight to his earthly cage, afraid to let the Spirit see the confusion and corruption that was within. With Christ's cleansing and an incorruptible body, he now could let loose of his former grasp, opening his soul's door as wide as God had made it. He learned quickly to throw open that door at every moment. Having no kingdom thing to fear, he could let in everything that the kingdom had to offer. God was glad at every moment to walk right through his open door to sit down and converse with him. He felt only constant companionship, walking as he was in locked arms not only with his Lord and Savior but also with his best friend. He was so thankful simply for being able at every moment to relate so closely to the Lord.

Blessing

"You have granted us unending blessings." Psalm 21:6.

PRAYER

We thank you, Father, for your endless blessings. You bless us with breath so that we rise in the morning. You bless us with a mind right to countenance you and your spectacular creation. You bless us with function to engage the world to satisfy both need and desire. You bless us a hundred ways, then a thousand, then ten thousand. Never-ending goods fall freely from your hands for us, all in witness of you. You could have made a world without blessing, one in which we felt nothing of your thought, nothing of your generosity. Instead, you chose to favor us, to treat us with a grace that we could not claim and rewards that were not ours to earn. You rained on us early, and you rained on us late, that our gardens would grow a hundred times what little that we planted. You brought forth a bounty beyond anything that we could dream. Your bounty was not material comfort, although of that you give us plenty, but rather was you. Father, we thank you that you chose to favor us, that you deigned to show us your grace. We thank you that when you favored us, you did so more richly than any favor any one of us could show one another. You blessed us so richly that we would know that our true benefactor was solely you. You are the giver of all goodness, the God who blesses in abundance beyond compare.

Answer

You know me as giver because I am your gift. You see the blessings that I shower down on you not as your earnings or other due but as my desire for you. When you thank me as gift giver, you favor me over my gifts. You honor me as your desire above everything that I give you. You are blessed because you know me, the one who blesses, rather than because you receive my gifts. Those who receive my gifts without acknowledging me as their giver have missed the point of my giving. They place their sustenance above my countenance. They value their life above my glory. No one who values their life above the life that I give them through my Son will save their life. They will lose their life because they credited the gifts that they believe sustain them, when instead I sustain them as their gift giver. Continue to thank me. Thank me when you rise and when you rest. Thank me when you receive my gifts and when you are still in want of them. Let your thanks be as abundant as my gifts, and then I will always know that you think more of me, your giver, than you do of the gifts. You will then have life, eternal life, in the joy of my kingdom. And because you have thanked me for abundant blessings, I will continue to pour them out to you, just as much as you thank me. I will show you my new blessings that are not of the kind that you formerly saw as my only or primary gifts. You will learn that I give other gifts to those who thank me in abundance. Let your thanks be generous, and I will show you things new.

Transformation

She saw God's blessing everywhere she turned. That realization didn't mean that her life was a figurative bowl of cherries. Indeed, her life seemed just about as confused and even at times despairing as were the lives of others around her. If she had designed anew her own circumstance, then she would have changed some of the old designs. Yet her personal messes notwithstanding, God just seemed to shower down blessings around her. She saw him providing, comforting, uplifting, guiding, and vitalizing. She saw how constantly creative he remained in her opportunities and relationships. She saw how he brought things into being out of nothing, creating hope and then victory where all had been despair and defeat. She saw how perfectly he regulated her body and environment, and her institutions and labors. Yes, they got stirred all up in an often-toxic mix, but that was her doing and the doing of others around her. God didn't create her messes. God drew her forward and upward out of them, every day a new day of opportunity. She could start over every day knowing that the new day needn't bring the old day's troubles. God had pardoned her, and thus she could pardon, so that the new day would bring its abundant blessings unmarred by the old day's sorrows. She saw in this hope God's greatest blessing, which was the forgiveness that he extended in Jesus Christ. She would thank him for every blessing but thank him most of all for Jesus Christ.

REVELATION

For her as for every other resident, the kingdom had every possible blessing because the kingdom had God. She knew that God had blessed her richly on earth, although she had not often exhibited or even felt such gratitude. That nagging sense of need or want greater than what God had granted had been another of earth's illusions, she now figured. Her slight sense of being in constant need had kept her from seeing how constantly God had then provided. Kingdom life admitted no need. Its bounty was obvious. Her resurrected body did not gnaw at her as her former body had done with its flesh desires. With everything so surely supplied, she had neither temptation nor excuse to feel any self-pity, any tendency toward gripe, whine, or complaint. In that way, the kingdom unburdened her from another habit that she had hardly realized that she had practiced so diligently in her former life. Few things, if anything, had ever measured up to her exacting standards in her former home. She always had cause for concern or complaint. Those causes, concerns, and complaints had hidden God's great earthly bounty. She had walked with the Lord's Spirit but hardly taken notice or given thanks. She had instead seen only how things had not met her elusive standard. In the kingdom, God held the only standard. She took no measure of anything because everything was so plainly his, so perfectly formed, and so generously given. She instead had a constant sense of thankfulness, which was just one more blessing that he had relieved her of any illusion that she had less from him and of him than she wanted. Everything that he had was hers, and she had all of him.

Family

"God sets the lonely in families." Psalm 68:6.

PRAYER

Father, we thank you for family, for making for us a home among others with whom we share ancestry and affinity. We thank you especially for a home in its ideals like the home that you share with your glorious Son and precious Holy Spirit. We might reach life without family, but we depend on family for shelter, provision, and nurture, indeed for education, responsibility, and discipline. We owe these things and so many more to our origin family, just as we thus owe these things and so many more to you who divined family. We find your paternal and patriarchal attributes in our earthly fathers and grandfathers. We also find attributes of your care, domesticity, and love in our earthly mothers and grandmothers. Gloriously, we find the filial love of your Son in our earthly brothers and sisters. We aspire to treat our children as you treat us, with patience, perseverance, and correction, together with care and generosity, but above all with your sacrificial love. The family that you promise and portend gives us a fighter's chance of becoming the kind of persons that you would have us become. Through family, we can live the kind of life that you would have us live. Even as family challenges us, we take comfort and pleasure in family, and draw humor and joy from family, all as gifts from you. Then, Father, after having blessed us with our natural family, you invite us to join your holy family, for which we thank you the most. Our natural family would not be the blessing that it is without our being brothers and sisters, sons and daughters, in your holy family. We are at home with you.

ANSWER

I blessed you with family that you would not feel alone in the world. I am always with you. I show you my love through the love of my Son and those who love with him. I created your family to show you how my Son loves. As parents and siblings, you are to love like my Son loved. Then your family will be my blessing. You will be at home with me when your family reflects the love of my Son. You must show the love of my Son within your family. Provide for your family with your labors, and bless your family with my word, while showering your family with my Son's love. You should also see the love of my Son in the generosity, grace, and mercy that your family shares with you. Receive, even as you give. In both giving and receiving, see the love of my Son. I am family, Father and Son joined in Spirit. Your family should show my family's love. My Spirit is at work in your family. Listen to my Spirit for how your family should work. Let my Spirit renew minds, transforming your family as my Spirit transforms you. Your family must not look like other families who do not welcome my Spirit. Because your family welcomes my Spirit, your family will take on the image of my family, where all is love. And because you thank me for family, I will indeed send my Spirit to transform your family as a witness to me and to my endless love. Your home will be like my home. Your family will love one another and show love to others as my Son has loved.

TRANSFORMATION

He had both an old family and a new family, pretty much as he had an old self and a transformed new life. Just as God had saved him from himself, giving him new birth and new life, so too, God had saved his family, giving his family new birth and new life. His old family had played its traditional role in nurture, provision, and education. He hadn't had a bad family, although all families of the old traditional type are difficult. His family had raised him, provided for him, and even in part educated him, although the greater part of his education was his own. Despite its provision, his family had been difficult, like all old-type families are difficult, and for which he too, still in his old self, was to blame. His new family, though, was not difficult. His new family constantly blessed him, even in surprising ways, not just the old ways. His new family took the Spirit as guide, and the Spirit guided his new family into riches of love that his old family could not and did not provide. His new family had a horizon far beyond his old family's sight. His new family looked beyond its natural end and into eternity. He thanked God daily for the Spirit and love of his new family, even as he thanked God for caring for members of his old family in their obstinate ignorance. He also thanked God for lifting him out of his own obstinate ignorance from his old family and into his new. He treasured being a member of God's family, a child of God and brother of Christ.

REVELATION

The kingdom meant family. Everywhere he looked, he saw brothers and sisters, sons and daughters. Everyone shared the lineage of Christ.

Everyone was familiar, just like family. Everyone had the experience and outlook of being a child of God and sibling to Christ. He could take a meal with anyone and feel entirely at home, while making others feel right at home, too. Anywhere two or more gathered, they gathered as family. He could wave to anyone, hail anyone, greet anyone, and they would always acknowledge him back not like a stranger but just like family. He had an instant bond with everyone whom he encountered. That bond included instant trust, automatic confidence, and certainty that the other submitted just as he did to the Father while embracing the Son. Each kingdom resident was as unique as each had been in their former life, with different personalities, appearances, and mannerisms. Yet each kingdom resident had firmly resolved before entry that they were giving their life to the Lord for the life that the Lord was giving to them. They were all completely indebted to him, each thus with an equal debt that they owed him. Each expressed their love for their brother Christ differently, with each difference precious to their Lord. But each was on the same terms with the Father, obedient to his will, and Son, owing the Son their life. Each member of heaven's one family thus had equal place at the great table of eternal life. God heard each of their voices equally, as any father must treat all of his children. God answered each according to their desires of him. He was so glad to be in God's home not as trespasser or even as guest but as family member. He was home.

Discipline

"Offer your bodies as living sacrifices." Romans 12:1.

PRAYER

We thank you, Father, for your discipline because we know that you discipline only those who are your children, your own family. Without your discipline, we would be lawless rebels and renegades, beyond your authority, free to do as we pleased for our own good, which would be no good at all. We would be common rather than holy. We would be beyond your reach, an eyesore and stench to you. When you discipline us, we turn away from our unholy ways and to your holy ways. Rather than chafe under your discipline, we repent under the influence of your Holy Spirit. The cleansing blood of your Son then regains for us your Son's glorious righteousness. We take on your Son's image again, so welcome and alluring to you. You discipline us not because you desire hardness and suffering but so that you can embrace us again. The hard consequences that your discipline imposes humble us, making us able to reach for you again. Make us go back and confess our wrongs, beseeching again your forgiveness. Make us return what we have stolen and repair what we have destroyed. Make us honor you where we have usurped your honor and give you credit where we have your credit wrongfully claimed. Yes, we want your loving approval, Father, but we also need and thank you for your loving discipline.

ANSWER

I discipline you because you are my children. I want you to have more than those who are not my children have. I want you to be holier than those who are not my children are. They are common because they are unruly in their lack of discipline. I want you bearing virtue and holiness, those attributes that increase through refining discipline. My discipline corrects and uplifts, setting you on the path to my kingdom heights. Vain praise puffs up. It does not purify. Receive my chastisement willingly, without revolt or annoyance. I rebuke not to degrade and destroy but to build and lift up. You press forward in your physical exercise to preserve your natural strength and improve your natural health. So too, you should press forward under my discipline to preserve your eternal life and improve your eternal reward. You rightly embrace my discipline, which though hard, yet means far more to you than the ease of commendation and confidence of praise. Let others praise you while my discipline corrects and persuades. Do not ignore the consequences of your actions. They are my gift to your maturation. Think of those consequences, and change your actions for the better accordingly. Realize how I guide and chasten, letting the consistency of my responses transform your character. Do not do as others do, repeating their sin endlessly while expecting me to change their outcome. I do not change. My discipline reveals my reliable desires. I am constant in my discipline because I desire your holy devotion. And because you accept my discipline, I will make my will for you ever clearer that you need not look at my discipline in vain.

TRANSFORMATION

He had come recently to the realization that God disciplined through situations, including through people, even obstinate and difficult people. He had for as long as he could remember thought that people who frustrated him in his own designs, who stood in his way and even antagonized him when he was trying to do as he thought that he ought, were an unfortunate hardship to endure. Why couldn't they just change their meddlesome ways or at least get out of the way while minding their own business? Recently, though, he had come to see that difficult people were as much God's messengers as anyone else. Indeed, they might even be greater harbingers of God than the gentle and gracious folks whom all preferred. Of course, the difficult few didn't at all seem to be doing God's work at the time of their very ungracious interference. They seemed instead to be preventing the work at all, at least in the way that he thought that the matters with which they interfered should proceed. Why would God send them, when they were unable to justify their own cause for their interference? He thought of Balaam's donkey stubbornly protecting his rider prophet who failed to see the angel on guard. Slow down, he thought, when you see someone acting like a stubborn donkey, slowing the initiative. Reassess your course, he realized, when a seemingly irrational person or incongruous circumstance stands in the path. Perseverance past the animate or inanimate object may be appropriate, but then again, the animate or inanimate may be doing God's work. Watch for God's discipline, he discerned, especially when having a full head of steam on one's own course. Do not call God's discipline down on one's own head, he determined, when God cautioned that he wait. Be a willing hand, but let God initiate the work.

Revelation

He realized in his kingdom residency that one thing of which earth had much and the kingdom had little was discipline. Not long had passed in his new kingdom residency when he lost entirely that old sense of foreboding, as if something was about to crash. The old crashes had of course just been critical instances of correction. Every crash had required of him a change in course, of which he had many. Indeed, he had formerly had so many of the same crashes that he had felt as if he had nearly grown immune to discipline, which had been a frightening thought. Would he ever learn? Would God soon give him up for lost, as no longer a child worthy of discipline but as an illegitimate reprobate? God had not given up on him because God could not forsake his own Son with whom the new resident had so closely associated as Savior, brother, and family. So the discipline had simply continued until he had breathed his last on earth. While he might have thought that the discipline would have resumed in the kingdom, God quite clearly had no such need or thought. The kingdom had no crashes. Its residents needed no further correction, having already had just enough chastisement, reprimand, and rebuke to guide them on their way to kingdom relief. In the end, he and every other resident had held fast to Christ. Discipline had done its work on earth. Thanks to that discipline, he and every other resident had each claimed Christ's victory as their own. The kingdom meant celebration, not further rebuke. Rebukes would instead continue their important work on earth, guiding the lost to their own victory in Christ.

Trials

"Consider it pure joy whenever you face trials of many kinds." James 1:2.

PRAYER

We thank you, Father, for the many trials that you permit to come our way. We know that you permit only those trials that cast us back on our faith in you. You restrain from us the whirlwind. If you let everything come our way, then we would not survive beyond a moment. You restrain life-threatening disease, mental and emotional distress, loved ones lost, relationships ruined, physical hardship, material want, liberties lost, and simple moment-to-moment frustrations and deprivations. Life's challenges would crush us without your protection from the vast bulk of them. You constantly hold certain defeat at bay. Yet you let through to us just those trials that you know will test and strengthen our faith. You know that we cannot grow stronger in faith without exercising it, and so you give our puny faith just that progressive degree of exercise that you know it can withstand. We are so thankful, Father, that you allow us these tests. Without them our hope and trust in you, our reliance on your grace and mercy, would remain stunted and weak, things of disgrace rather than honor. We want your generous reward when we enter your kingdom. We know that life's trials will earn that reward for us by refining and increasing our faith. We always have you, oh Father, and so we endure trials of every kind knowing that they do not move you one step farther from us but instead draw us closer to you. Thank you for these trials, Father, for every one of them. You have your purpose in letting them come, even as you shelter us from a multitude of others. Continue to strengthen our faith through them.

Answer

You are right to celebrate when you face trials that are both of your making and of mine. You would have no cause to prove your faith without them. Faith unexercised is either weak faith or no faith at all. When you face a trial, your faith stands forth. In trials, especially severe trials, you turn to me and rely on me. Trials show you that your own defenses are weak, your fortresses made of sticks. You must in your trials depend on my strength, which I can only make evident to you when you realize your weakness. Trials require you to endure in faith, to know that I rescue the weary and oppressed. I do not serve the strong like false gods relying on human ingenuity and human strength. I instead stand of my own accord, without your help. I ask only that you endure in trials so that you can see me shut the lion's mouth and quell the murderous horde. Trials give you every reason to fear, for such is their design. Trials desire that you give in and give up, that you succumb to fear in sacrifice of your faith. I ask only that you wait patiently for my deliverance. Do not turn away from me in trials. Know that I will come. Wait until it looks like your end. I control your destiny. You have eternal life with me. When you have lost all else, then persevere still in my strength. And because you have thanked me for trials, I will go before you in trials in ways that you can see. You will no longer fear my absence. I will no longer hide my power from you, nor from your enemies. You will see me carry the battle for you in trials, with victory assured in the resolve and resurrection of my Son.

Transformation

She could see her times of testing coming from a long way off. They never failed to arrive. She didn't welcome any of them. How could one welcome what one could barely endure? She shuddered at the thought of the next one of them. The only thing that she knew was that she would last through every one of them. While they were almost too much to think about because almost too much to bear, she had faith that God would carry her through every one of them. While every one of them was a match for her, none of them were a match for her Savior. She clung to him through trials because he ruled all trials. He had long ago won. She knew that she had only to endure in her weak faith because her Savior was matchlessly strong. She thus didn't particularly regret trials after they had passed. She was not a whiner and complainer. Indeed, instead, after every trial, she felt the thrill of another victory won. She loved watching her Savior do battle, knowing the successful outcome. She especially loved when her Savior did battle for her, which only occurred in her trials. In that respect, she felt the joy of trials, even if trials themselves were no joy. She was closest to her Savior when she was most in need of him. Trials were those times. She only looked forward to the day when he had won her last battle and all was bliss. In eternity, she would face no more trials, only the sweet taste of his utter victory won.

REVELATION

Another kingdom feature that sustained her great joy and filled her with gratitude was that the kingdom presented no trials. Trials had weighed down her former life. She had the joy of the Lord inside but had a hard time showing that joy when trials challenged her daily. Some trials were small, while others were large, indeed some very large. She might have been able to face any one of them, even the big ones, without losing her joy and gratitude. Yet cumulatively, they had a burdensome effect. They pressed her down, forcing her to exercise her faith, which she knew then was their point. In the kingdom, though, she faced no trials. Every activity presented itself not as a test of her faith but as an opportunity to worship the ever-present and all-loving God. She had no longer to examine her faith, correct her complaints, and forge ahead through trials. She had already proven her faith, which was simply reliance on the perfect faith and completed work of her Savior. The kingdom presented no tests because that Savior was present in his glory, and every resident had met the entrance test. Every resident had relied on the Son passing the one great test. The Son had completed his steadfast trek to the cross, receiving in return the Father's glory in resurrection. She had embraced the Son's victory as her own. The Father had accepted her into his kingdom as his own daughter under the cover of his Son. Now, all that she did from moment to moment was to give God the joy and honor that his plan had won. The training and tournaments were over. Everything was now victory celebration. The Son had won, she had passed the last test, and the trials were over.

Service

"Offer your bodies as living sacrifices." Romans 12:1.

PRAYER

We thank you, Father, for the opportunity, will, and capacity to serve. We know that giving is better than receiving. Thank you, Father, for allowing us to give and serve, for planning our good works in advance. You alone have equipped us with the skill and function to do those good works. You then bring those good works to our attention for us to accomplish with the resources that you also provide. Under these providential circumstances, we give you the credit for any good that we manage to do. Keep letting us serve, oh Lord, so that we may give more than we receive, even though we receive so much and also know that when giving we do receive. We know that all, whether giving or receiving, is from you. Keep bringing those good works to our attention, keep increasing our capacity and skill. Keep us faithful to do the good work that you plan for us and present to us to do. We ask these things in prayer, not that others would serve us but that we would serve others, because we know our debt of gratitude to you. We know how you have blessed us especially within the service that we do. We know that we are capable to serve only because you give us the life, discernment, and means to so do. Even more so, you give us your Spirit of service, your Son's sacrificial love in which he came and conquered not for himself but to bring us back to you. We thus thank you, Father, for your Son's service, even as we thank you for our own ability and will to serve. Your Son was the servant King, and so we aspire to serve.

ANSWER

You pray wisely that my Son was your servant and is now your King. You indeed serve because he served you. You are wise in your gratitude for your ability and will to serve others. Many want others to serve them, while my people want to serve others, knowing my servant will. Your service does not diminish you as others would assume. Your service shows you strong, capable, and generous, not lacking in character and will. You have the heart of my Son when you serve others. Your service turns others to my Son when they see his service in you. You do not draw anyone to me when you expect others to serve you. My leaders, so like my servant Son, are those who serve, not those who desire that others serve them. Increase your heart for service. Do not let your hands be idle when you see others to whom you can ably attend. Move swiftly to their aid. Give generous service, not meager service. Serve in kindness, forgiving others' ignorance of your service and their high-minded expectation that only you, and not they, should serve. My Son died for having served and yet prayed that I would forgive those who condemned him. My Son made the cross your symbol of service. Bear your cross generously, for in giving so generously, you will generously receive. You will receive eternal life. And because you have thanked me for your ability and opportunity to serve, rather than for others serving you, I will make of you a servant leader, one to whom others look for the loving service of my Son.

TRANSFORMATION

She drew such pleasure from service that she nearly felt it odd to do so. Oh, she supposed that she felt the same pains and frustrations that anyone did when running the mundane errands that comprise most effective service. She didn't see or sense anything grand in the errands themselves. She wasn't saving a drowning child, adopting an orphan, curing cancer, or feeding a starving village. Her service was ordinary rather than grand, the small things that might make a person's life a little better and easier. She also didn't get much appreciation from those whom she served, not that they were ungrateful. Her pleasure wasn't in the service acts, the thanks that they garnered, or even in the benefit to the people. Instead, she seemed to draw her pleasure from growing closer to Christ. Service removed barriers, particularly the obstacles of her own needs and wants. When she was serving, she was thinking of him and pursuing his desire rather than thinking of herself and pursuing her own desire. Her service left few or no regrets. She gained nothing material in her service, which just convinced her all the more that her reward would be in heaven. Her reward would be the heart of Christ. She loved the worship services where she often felt his Spirit near. Yet she loved her quiet service to others even more, where his heart felt to her assured. She knew that he was nearest when she served because she followed a servant Lord.

REVELATION

The kingdom held for her a different kind of service than that to which her Lord had called her on earth. She soon realized in her kingdom residency that as much as she had enjoyed it, her earthly service had remained a yearning for her Lord. She had at times felt that his Spirit had so clearly guided her that the Lord worked with her. Yet those times were rare. She had more often questioned whether she was truly doing the Lord's work. Maybe instead, she was just interfering with and even disabling others who needed to face their own consequences, proving their own faith. Maybe others were better at the work than she, she often thought when her service work didn't exactly turn out as she had hoped. Maybe the Lord wanted her doing other work than the work that she chose for its ease and convenience. She had also wondered about her motives, whether she was doing the work for the notice it might bring her rather than because she loved to please the Lord. So her service on earth had been like everything else there, incomplete and confusing, a mix of the common and the holy in which she had never been sure of his approval. The kingdom in its clarity withheld no approval. She knew the Lord's will because he was present in person to share it with her. While the Spirit had on earth spoken in whispers to ensure that she would seek the Lord to follow him into the kingdom, the Lord in heaven spoke plainly. She could do his will knowing exactly what he wanted from her. Service in the kingdom, though, was different in another way. No resident lacked anything. No resident had the burden of sin and corruption. Everything that she did for another was clearly an act of love for that other and for the Lord. He had already provided. She was only sharing with others that which he had already shared with her. She was so grateful for the clarity, generosity, and pure motives of her modest kingdom service, so unlike her former uncertain service life.

Beauty

"Your beauty is that of a gentle and quiet spirit." 1 Peter 3:4.

PRAYER

We thank you, Father, for beauty, symmetry, order, art, pattern, and proportion. We thank you for all of those visual, aural, and tactile splendors that you bring into the world. You have surrounded us with such exquisite designs, organic and inorganic, all animated by your holiness, your otherworldliness and divinity. You bring these elegances to our attention to remind us of you, your desire for ordering things according to your purpose and will. In beauty, we see the best of your function and structure, those things through which your providence blesses us. Your beautiful natural order allows us to create in your honor. We aspire to imitate your art and order, and in doing so to turn attention to you. Yet you are the artist, the painter, sculptor, and performer. You dazzle us with the possibilities of perfection that inhere in your creation. We even see beauty in humans whom you made in your image, though particularly the beauty of your own chosen people in their gentle and quiet spirits so like that of your wondrous Son. Indeed, we most desire to gaze on your beauty, on your form and face incarnate in your Son. Your beauty reminds us of the hope with which we live. We anticipate your eternal kingdom in which everything will be your splendor. Continue to bless us with your stunning and gorgeous creations that we may always look up and forward to you.

ANSWER

While you do well to celebrate the beauty of my creation, you have seen only a small portion of my work, a glimmer of all the beauty that I command. My designs are so many and exquisite that I have realms that you haven't imagined, splendors that you cannot comprehend. You are not yet ready to see more of the splendor of my creation until my Spirit clears and enlarges your mind. Your eyes can only see so little, and your ears can so little yet hear. I have things to show you that you must wait to see until my Spirit prepares your soul, sight, and mind. The sight of those things too early would confuse, confound, and compromise your unprepared mind. My Son fed thousands from nothing, raised the dead, and walked from his own grave resurrected, things that you cannot explain and that you barely accept. Why should I trust you with more of my gorgeous designs? See first that which I have done and your own witnesses have duly recorded. Then I will show you more of my work up to your own resurrection. Imagine your sibling or spouse resurrected, or even your own child. Then you will know the full wonder of my loving enterprise. Imagine the unimaginable, and you will still have fallen short of my endless possibilities. I do not simply create. I marshal beauty, rule, and order. My work makes you possible while also making possible your own creations. You say truly that your meager works, so splendid to your own minds, can do no better than honor me, who gave you meaning and mind. You are conscious of the beauty of my creation only because I gave you sight, hearing, sense, and mind. And because you have honored the beauty of my creation, I will indeed prepare you to see more. You will see splendor previously unknown.

Transformation

He was from a family of artists who did not know God. He had no art, but he had God, while his family had art but no God. He saw beauty, order, symmetry, and design in the art that his family members created, although he saw far more of those things and many other things in the art and designs of God. He knew further that God had only shown him a glimpse of his own designs, while his family members were showing their all. Indeed, he knew that his family members made art only with the materials that God supplied and only with the eye that God designed. He wished that his family members would see their debt and honor their creator with their designs. They didn't do so overtly, having no confession to make of Christ and so no knowledge of the image and love of God. Yet he hoped perhaps that God saw their subtle confession in the modest designs of their art. He also prayed diligently that their art would lead them to the one who enabled it, the uncreated creator who gave the created the passion to create. He prayed that they would see God in their own art if not in God's infinitely greater art, indeed, in the odd beauty and humble majesty of their own humankind. They, too, had his nobility within them. He could not create as his family members created, for God had not blessed him with the gift of art. God had instead blessed him to see God in art, toward which he again turned his earnest prayer that his family members would share the same blessing. Would, after all, one rather make one's own humble art alone or live forever in the family of the greatest artist?

Revelation

The kingdom instantly impressed every new resident with its extraordinary beauty, just as it had impressed him. The great wonder of the place was to lead its residents constantly on looking for another glorious expression of God's love for them all. The kingdom cared so perfectly for him and all others that he felt as if he was continually on God's mind, which of course he was. He always had been, even on earth, although on earth his own sin and corruption had led him to chase many illusions. The kingdom's care was evident in everything from food to shelter to comfort. That care was not just ordinary, either, but instead lavish, at all times reminding him that the Father cared for him as he cared for his own Son. Earth, too, had been beautiful, but earth had also been ugly, hard, and dangerous. He had seen God then in earth's beauty, but he had also seen how sin and corruption marred earth's beauty and hid God. The kingdom wasn't like earth in that respect at all. Nothing marred the kingdom's beauty, which at all times fully reflected the perfection of a glorious God. Unlike on earth, in the kingdom he could see something alluring from afar and trust that on his approach and close inspection, it would look even more beautiful. The kingdom's beauty, too, was of all kinds, from the grand and spectacular to the exquisitely fine. The kingdom's beauty bathed the residents in God's glory like a continually healing balm. He had often been thankful on earth for the splendor of God's creation. In the kingdom, that gratitude swelled into continual song.

Vocation

"Live a life worthy of the calling you have received." Ephesians 4:1.

PRAYER

We thank you, Father, for vocation, for occupation and employment. We thank you even for our identity as ones called to specific works. Your word identifies apostles as tentmakers, fishermen, and tax collectors. So, too, may you and others identify us by the vocations and careers in which you call us to engage, even as you simultaneously see in us the light of your Holy Spirit. We thank you that you have given us vocations through which to plow both material and spiritual fields. We thank you for letting us earn our keep here while earning our kingdom reward for later. Through the generous capacities with which you bless us, Father, let our fair and fruitful commerce provide for ourselves and our families. Lord, let it also generate a healthy surplus to provide for those who cannot do so for themselves. We thank you for that surplus, that you enable our labors to generate goods for others as well as for ourselves. Help us to see in our occupation not just the opportunity to acquire and amass but to share and supply. Do not let us identify so closely with our occupations that we do not identify with you. While you call us to vocation, we know that our ultimate identity is not in our earthly labor but in the mission of your Son. Our true vocation is in service of your grander designs. So, Father, continue to call us to vocations in which we can do your will, shining the light of your Son on all those whom we serve, that all may know and love you.

ANSWER

You do well to ply the vocations that I give you, as if you worked for me. Indeed, you do work for me. Even as you lean to your labors feeling like ordinary beasts of burden, your labors also serve my greater design. Your labors bring your co-worker and those whom your generous work supplies closer to me. They see in your commitment to produce and provide the greater service of my Son. Everything that you do in your vocation reflects my Son. When you rise early to your labors, they see my Son's enterprise. When you labor long, they see my Son's light yoke. When you labor through challenges, they see my Son's perseverance. When you labor gladly, they see my Son's joy. When you labor keenly, they see my Son's discernment. When your labors innovate, they see my Son's creativity. Vocation is your ministry field, especially when you also share generously the salvation mission of my Son. Do not hide my Son's role in the satisfaction of your labors. Let all who benefit from your work know its vital source. Be sure that you do not labor for your own honor or reputation but for the credit that your labors bring to my Son. Share with your co-workers my Son's name and the eternal fruit of his labor so that your own work will not be in vain. If in your vocation you honor my Son, then your reward will not be temporary but eternal. When your vocation runs out, you will have stored up much in heaven. And because you have thanked me for vocation, I will bless your vocation with the special ministry of my Son as you desire. Your vocation will reflect my Son to my credit.

TRANSFORMATION

He had always taken satisfaction in work that provided for himself and his family. God had first given him a strong back and later a strong mind, each in its own time serving to earn ample income. With God's generosity always evident, his labors provided for his own and for others. He could see working this way into old age largely for the satisfaction of the work's material supply. Yet despite the work's material satisfaction, he still feared that his labors were not all that God expected him to supply. He wanted to connect his work to God's grand design. He didn't want to be working for things that rust and spoil but for things that last, indeed for eternal reward. He had no explicit ministry. His vocation was common, not one that others associated with eternity. He thought a little about changing his vocation to an explicit ministry. Somehow, though, he felt that God had not called him away from his long-term vocation as much as to reexamine it. In doing so, he saw how God could shape that vocation to grander designs, things that touched on his Son's salvation mission, things that earned eternal reward. And so he prayed not just in thanks for having vocation's material supply but also that God would give him bold words and actions of witness within his vocation. He wanted his co-workers and others with whom his vocation brought him into contact to know the real reason for his diligent work. He wanted them to know Christ the servant and savior Lord. Let his labors be for his own and others' eternal reward.

REVELATION

He had in his former life occasionally wondered what vocation would be like in heaven. Work had been such a big part of his former life, as it was for most others. He sensed then that he identified too much with work and not enough as a child of God. He wanted God to identify and define him for his own peace of mind and for its testimony to others. Yet work in his former life had so challenged and at times burdened or consumed him that he found it difficult to manage. Work had always been either too much or too little, too easy or too hard. Work had always meant doing some of the right thing but more of the wrong thing, pleasing some while displeasing others. Kingdom work was different, though. He could really say that the kingdom had no work because no one earned anything by the sweat of any brow. No one labored to supply one's self or to supply another because God had supplied all. Vocation was instead entirely creative, as in a sense he had always wanted it to be in his former life. The best of vocation on earth seemed to have been when it reflected the joy, skills, and interests of the workers, which was seldom if ever true. By contrast, kingdom work was always joyful work, always reflecting the skills and passions of its participants. Moreover, kingdom work was always godly work, always done solely to honor God. Kingdom work never reflected avarice, covetousness, materialism, or greed, as it so often did on earth. He worked in the kingdom, in effect tending God's endlessly rich garden. God granted him a unique kingdom vocation that drew on the talents with which God had blessed him to honor God. Yet his kingdom work never interfered in the least with his devotion to God. His kingdom identity was far more than as a worker of a certain kind. He finally had the full identity that God had always intended for him as a child of God.

Life

"In him was life, and that life was the light of all humankind." John 1:4.

PRAYER

We thank you, Father, for life. We thank you simply for the breath and consciousness of living. We find it wondrous that we know who we are, that we are aware of our own identity and thinking. We find it even more wondrous that others are equally conscious of us and of themselves, that we share a world of sentient beings. Still more wondrous is that we know who *you* are. Thank you, Lord, that you have given us the will to choose whom to follow, whether you, ourselves, or another. Your glory would be no less had you made only robots and automatons to serve you. Yet you brought us, as willful creatures, into your universe. You made us conscious of that universe and our place in it. You granted us the ability to shape the world for better or worse. You made us little gods, much as you, our one great God, are your universe's conscious designer. Life, we know, lies in you alone. While some think that they have their own life, self-imbued, we know instead that life is not inherent in us. You imbued us with your life, breathing into us your Spirit. We have life for only as long and only on the terms that you choose for us. We are eternally grateful that you granted us life, especially in that you have given us the choice of your eternal life. Having given us will to choose, you have also given us knowledge of the tree of life, indeed access to that tree. You have given us eternal life through your savior Son. We thank you, Father, that you did not just set us alive and leave us with mortal life and thus morbid life. We thank you that you also breathed us alive with your Spirit, giving us life anew, transformed life in coming resurrected body.

ANSWER

You have life because I live in person and Spirit, and I love and am love. When I create, I also imbue with my life and Spirit. I do not make merely the inanimate. I do not create merely mortal beings. Because I live, breathe, and move eternally, you too live, breathe, and move with will for the eternal. I made you in my image. My image is not a lifeless and mechanical thing. My image is living flesh infused with Spirit. Because I am conscious, thinking, and intending, so you also think and intend. You could not honor me if you lacked choice and will. I gave life, Spirit, and will to you in order that you would choose to pursue, discover, and honor me. No creator creates for the creator's own dishonor. I cannot deny myself. My creatures must have the opportunity to see me, know me, and glorify me. I sent my Son to accomplish that mission, to reveal me to my creatures in order that they would join me for my glory. I desire that all would live and none perish. My desire that all would live is why I sent my Son and why he lived, died, and lived again as he did. I sent my word to you that you would know how you might live as I live, into eternity. I desire eternity for all. You know well that you need only submit to my Son to join me in eternity. When my Son lived, died, and lived again, he created the portal and pattern through which you too would live forever. The life that I gave you I intended to be eternal life. You need not perish. Submit to my Son, accepting his salvation and following his path into eternity. Then you will glorify me forever. And because you have thanked me for life, I will give you abundant life even into eternity.

TRANSFORMATION

She could feel God's life within her. She supposed that she had her own natural life. She could just barely imagine God leaving her to her own life, but at the same time she knew that she would not be long for the world if that were so. No, God's Spirit kept her going. The Holy Spirit lived within her. She knew so in part because she could see the Spirit in others. She could see the Spirit in their eyes, in their energy, in their smiles and laughter, and sometimes even in their seriousness. Oh, the words, life, and actions of others always hid the Spirit at least a little. No one looked to her quite like Jesus must have looked, completely at one with the Spirit. She couldn't imagine anyone else suddenly transfigured, as God transfigured Jesus. Yet she could still see the Spirit delightfully at work in others, even if in some more than in others. Because she could see the Spirit in others, she could feel the Spirit in herself. She nurtured this feeling, hoping that in doing so she was welcoming the Spirit. She didn't want the Spirit to depart. She knew that her life depended on the Spirit's presence. She prayed that God would continue to bless her richly with his Spirit. She wanted the Spirit leading her into eternal life.

REVELATION

She knew immediately that kingdom life was life as God wished her to live it. From her first kingdom moment, she felt strangely more alive than she had ever truly felt in her former life. The sensation was some combination of energy restored, burden lifted, and veil removed. Whatever the difference was, she had so much more vitality, such greater acuity of her senses, and such a clearer mind that in her resurrected body she felt as if she had entirely new life. Of course, she did have new life, free from every decay, decline, and corruption with which her former life had burdened her. Yet although she might have guessed that the kingdom would give her new energy and that her resurrected body would feel like her old body renewed, she had not anticipated that the difference would be so great. Indeed, she could accomplish things physically that she had never before imagined. She could see and hear things that she had never before seen or heard. She even considered the possibility that besides its evident incorruption, the kingdom wasn't all that different from earth, only that its residents had such greater abilities and acuities. The place was such a living marvel in part because its residents had such life to enjoy it. Paradise would be nothing of the sort if one were disabled from enjoying it. In the kingdom, every resident had full ability to explore and enjoy its paradise. Although God would have delighted her simply by restoring her youthful strength and health, she reveled in her newfound abilities. Resurrection was everything that Jesus's several appearances had intimated that it would be. Her incorruptible body gave her uncorrupted abilities and life.

Fellowship

"God has called you into fellowship with his Son." 1 Corinthians 1:9.

PRAYER

We thank you, Father, for fellowship. We thank you for friendship and companionship but particularly for fellowship in faith, in your church, and in your Son. We are each so different while also so isolated from one another. Our bodies imprison us. Our own thoughts, emotions, needs, and desires consume us within them. Loneliness is our natural condition. These fleshly vessels ensconce and encapsulate us so remotely from one another. We thus find authentic friendship and companionship rare and difficult to maintain. We need relationships where we feel the constant supporting presence of another, one who is somehow sufficiently alike in affinity to ourselves. We are fortunate to have one friend in a hundred acquaintances. Yet through fellowship in faith, we find a wide circle of friends who also choose to pursue your Son and accept his pursuit of us. We speak different languages and dialects, have different backgrounds and experiences, and have distinct skills and tastes. Still, you give us brothers and sisters in Christ, others with whom we share fundamental truth and commitments. Where, when, or how we encounter another of your followers does not matter, for in every such encounter we find fellowship in your Spirit. We are never alone when among your followers, Father, and so for that eternal and most-trustworthy fellowship, we thank you.

ANSWER

You live among my followers, each of you with me in common. When you share me, you can know and trust one another. You can see my Spirit in you and among you. You have reason and rationale to relate to one another, and not merely to satisfy your needs but to celebrate my glory. You share generous hope and a glorious future. Without me, you have no fellowship. You are alone, each to your own desires. Your pasts alienate you, and your futures divide you. You have no common end to pursue and no hope for a future. You live in despair, unable to comfort one another, and instead opposed to one another. In me, you have unity of thought, goal, and purpose. I draw you up and forward together, a blessed faith fellowship proceeding together into eternity. You support and encourage one another along your common path, while inviting others to join you. Yours is a happy procession, daily growing larger by the joy it spreads among those others. You live in celebratory parade, your own daily tasks coordinate with the tasks and activities of others in march toward my kingdom. You find companionship that you would not otherwise have. Your walls become bridges. You lay down your weapons to take the plowshare together, sowing my fertile fields. And because you have thanked me for granting you the fellowship of my Spirit, I will fill your path with many more faith friends with whom you may travel joyfully.

TRANSFORMATION

She had, as she thought of it, many faith friends. She knew that in nearly every instance, they would not have been friends if they had not shared her faith. She was not aloof or selective in that respect. She would befriend anyone who wished to share life's journey. She just found that as one proceeded on that journey, paths diverged. Those of her faith fellowship stuck to the same path, while others chose other paths. She would walk for a time along the same path with acquaintances who were outside her faith fellowship or whose faith she did not know and perhaps they also did not know. But in those cases, paths diverged in time. Her longtime friends were faith friends, sticking to the sojourner's path in fellowship, in this temporary home on their way to their eternal home in God's kingdom. She was deeply thankful for these faith friends. A few were nearly constant companions, while others she saw only occasionally or even rarely. Yet each seemed like a beacon for her, lighting her path forward once again on their common journey to the kingdom. Her life would have been different without her companions, much more challenging, empty of the joy and laughter that she shared with them. She knew that she always had the Lord with her. These friends, though, carried the joy of the Lord. She was glad that he had imbued them with that joy, so evident of his light Spirit. She hoped also that she was a joy and beacon to them.

REVELATION

The kingdom confirmed and vastly expanded for her the fellowship that she had in small respects enjoyed in her former life. The kingdom had many other residents, each of whom had like her dedicated their lives to honor Father through Son. They were all of one accord, which meant everything to her in trusting in their fellowship. Because every resident shared her own singular commitment and thus her only significant affinity, she never lacked not only for company but also for companionship. She found that every happy resident whom she encountered could be an instant companion. No fellowship did anything other than lift and encourage its every member. No gathering devolved to anything less than the full trust and enjoyment of every member. Every assembly left the participants assured of the common joy and mission of its every member, which was to celebrate the generous glory of God. Every member had the same Savior, and so every member had the same core testimony to give, even though the experience of each member had been different. She loved every encounter, whether planned or fortuitous. Every encounter brought her another glad companion. No resident burdened, confused, or distracted another, even those who had shared unhappy fellowship in their former lives. No memory of those former lives strained any relationship because God's good purpose in every interaction was now clear and accomplished. She felt her joy growing with every such relief over old relationships. She also felt her fellowship gradually growing into the kingdom's expanse as she met and got to know more of its loving and encouraging residents. Perhaps best of all, she could see that she encouraged others as much as they encouraged her. Their mutual commitment to the glory of God in Christ assured their mutual contagious affection. She was so grateful for the fellowship of the kingdom's residents.

Redemption

"God's grace justifies all freely through Jesus Christ." Romans 3:24.

PRAYER

We cherish you, Father, for redemption. You have cared for us so deeply. You have delivered us from tremendous weight, the unbearable burden of our ingrained venality and vice. Your Son's sacrifice clove us into two selves. Our old self is now forever dead in its sin, while our newborn self is forever alive in your image. Your Spirit continually breathes life into our transformed image. We listen to your Spirit speak your Son's life into and through our newborn image. We turn so gladly away from our wearying old self, knowing that it has no remaining life. We embrace the eternal life and divine purpose with which your Spirit imbues us. We have tired completely of battling the old life, reforming the old self. We have instead given up the old life for dead to accept your Son's new life. How can we do anything other than love and adore you, Father, for giving us this redeemed, newly born, and transformed life that your Holy Spirit continually refreshes? We give glory to you, Father, and glory to your Son and Spirit, for your redemptive work. We regard your work as wonder within wonder that you wrought divinity from the desolate. You have made of us a choir worthy to praise you, now that we have the standing of your own holiness. We revel in our new holiness that has removed the ancient barrier that our wickedness erected between us and you. Your Son opened heaven's door, through which we the redeemed rush, covered and cloaked in his gleaming attire, to fall at your knees in glad worship. Thank you, Father, for this richest redemption, giving us back to you. You are the redeemer, and we are your redeemed.

ANSWER

My Son's sacrifice redeemed you. His resurrection brought you back to me. You have his path before you. I rejoice that you embrace your redemption. I had lost you to your sin but desired you redeemed. I wanted you back with me. How was I to accomplish your redemption without giving something of greater value than the deep debts that you owed? The life of my Son was that greater value. I gave for you something that I could not give without losing my own life, requiring the blood and life of my own Son. To truly know me, you must embrace the inestimable cost of your redemption. You must see in that incalculable cost my inestimable love for you. I wanted you back, but I want you to know what getting you back cost me. Only by knowing redemption's cost will you know the depth and breadth of my love for you. Nothing but the cross could adequately reveal both redemption's love and cost. You should indeed thank me as you have done, although be sure that your gratitude approaches the depth of the debt that my Son paid. No gratitude less than your utter gratefulness could serve. And because you have thanked me in deepest gratitude, I will show you more of my redemptive love. I will reveal to you how thoroughly I have cleansed you of the stain of your transgressions. You will find yourself free of prior wrongs the guilt for which you didn't recognize still restrained you. You will cast off additional bonds and live in the liberty of my full absolution. The price that my Son paid was no less than your full price. Your gratitude in its depth frees you.

TRANSFORMATION

He carried burdens of his guilt that he was still discovering. Others didn't seem to carry burdens, although maybe they did and he, or they, just didn't know it. But he certainly carried those burdens. He hadn't noticed it at first. Only gradually did he realize that his past weighed on him, affecting both his present and his view of his future. He didn't so much begin each day fresh as begin each day beset by the prior day's burdens. He could hardly lift his head to see the horizon for all that the weight of yesterday's memories weighed on him. Every new day meant carrying more and more of yesterday's offenses. The burdens didn't dissipate but instead accumulated, every day adding transgressions. The only relief that he found was in thinking of Jesus. Somehow, what Jesus did on the cross relieved his guilt burden because *Jesus had said so.* The transgressions that weighed him down were apparently right there with Jesus. Jesus's suffering was paying the guilt that burdened him. He could not look at the offenses without depression and hopelessness, but he could look to Jesus with hope borne of forgiveness. He needed a pardon, and Jesus's suffering was giving it to him. The offenses were great and many, but Jesus's sacrifice was greater. He lived in a broken world, more broken because of his own actions within it, but Jesus had saved that world. Brokenness didn't matter so much anymore. Burdens had lifted. He could walk erect, clear his mind, and breathe more easily, especially anticipating joining Jesus.

REVELATION

He hadn't thought of it before his merciful entry, but he quickly discovered that the kingdom had to deal with his redemption before it could offer him resurrection. The kingdom dealt with redemption at his entry. He was not gaining the kingdom on any merit of his own. No resident did. No merit, however great, could satisfy a perfect God against whose glory all fall short. Jesus's sacrifice as the perfect Son of God offered the only key to the kingdom. Yet that he and others knew the Son as kingdom key was in itself ineffective. All entrants had first to grasp the key, which meant acknowledging before God and others their utter need of the Son. He had made this acknowledgment before others in his former life in many ways and settings. Still, he had no direct way of telling whether he had made the acknowledgment before God as God expected. Although he had called out to Jesus so many times, he still couldn't say with any certainty whether God truly knew him. In this respect, too, he had only God's promises on which to rely. He could not confirm his own passport. His last moment on earth and first moment approaching the kingdom's gate had exactly that quality. He was not going to stand before God self-justifying. He was going to throw himself once again, as he had so many times before, on God's own promises and mercy. God's greatest promise and mercy was Christ's sacrifice, which he took as his only sure footing for kingdom entry. As his former life ebbed away, he held fast to that one thought, only to realize in the next moment that he was holding to Christ in full embrace in the kingdom. The Father could not have parted them if he had wished, of which of course he had no desire, for he, too, was in Son's full embrace.

Resurrection

"'Who believes in me will live, even though they die.'" John 11:25.

PRAYER

We thank you, Father, for resurrection. We thank you for letting us know that we will live even though we die. You gave your dying Son life in order that relying on him we would live. When you opened heaven's ancient gates to your Son, those gates also opened for us to join you through him. We thus no longer live despairingly in these temporary tents. We instead live anticipating the glory of worshiping you in resurrected body. Through the hope of resurrection, you give us anticipation of unspeakable joy, tastes of boundless bliss bursting forth from your own eternity. You invite us to contemplate revival. You ask us to anticipate and embrace resurrection. You want us to have the courage that doing so gives us in the face of our own constantly evident mortality. You have broken death's grip not only on our bodies but on our souls. You have freed us not only from a future natural end but also present spiritual despair. Fatalism has no grip on us. We rise from despondency, shake off pessimism, and shrug off death and defeat. Your resurrection life turns our passivity into activity, resignation into resolve, and stoicism into eager anticipation and excitement. When your Son rose at your behest, you turned us giddy with the same hope. You have our eternal thanks, Father, for such joy in resurrection.

ANSWER

You whom I redeemed I also resurrected. I did not merely pay the debt that your sin accumulated, freeing you from its burden. I also opened heaven's gates that you may once again enter my presence. I brought you back to life as I brought my Son back to life. I raised you from the dead as I raised my Son from the dead. I broke death's grip on you, giving you access once again to eternal life. You may now live forever as my Son and I live forever. I will resurrect your dead body into a body that lives forever. I will restore the full function of your deceased mind. You will die your natural death at an hour and moment that you cannot predict, but I will raise you to life again, and not your natural life but to supernatural life of a kind that you have not yet experienced. I not only judge and discipline, but I also resurrect. I alone can make you whole, make you anew. You will not find the equal of resurrection in anything else that you can do. Do everything that you can to improve your lot now and to extend your life, but you will still die. No one other than I, and nothing else other than my Son's sacrifice, can promise you eternal life in transformed body. Accept my redemption and resurrection, and you will cry no more tears, feel no more pain, and suffer no more loss. Your resurrection will give you paradise in proximity to me.

Transformation

She read accounts and watched depictions of heaven eagerly. She trusted none of them but found all of them fascinating. She knew that she could not confirm how she would feel in resurrected life, but she also imagined that she might feel like any of the accounts and depictions. She might fly in heaven. She might run as swift as lightning and jump as high as mountains. She would feel love like she never quite felt it before. Her worn and broken body would be worn and broken no more. She would feel the energy of youth and the beauty of maturity. She would be able to move with ease from region to region. She would not tire but instead grow stronger. Her emotions would be constant joy, confidence, and generosity, never sadness and despair. She wouldn't stumble from crisis to crisis because heaven would hold no crises. She would shed no tears. Everything would be gladness and celebration. She would work without toil, create with doubt, and eat without hunger. Most of all, though, she would see the Lord like she had never quite seen him before. She imagined that she might even touch him, not that touch would even be necessary given his presence, immanence, and eminence all around her in heaven. Resurrection was going to be so special, she knew, that she could hardly wait for it. Until then, she would serve the Lord.

Revelation

The kingdom did far more than welcome her in her old condition. Indeed, the kingdom did something entirely different. The kingdom gave her what she had long known but little understood as *resurrection*. She knew that in heaven with her Lord, she would have an incorruptible body, one that still somehow was her own image but that had new life and capability. She knew so because the scriptures indicated that the Lord himself had a new body in resurrection from his marred and broken old one. She just hadn't anticipated how broken her old body was or in contrast how vivified would be her new one. That the scriptures recorded Christ readily appearing and disappearing, even passing easily in and out of locked rooms, suggested the powers of her own new body. These powers were things that she did not even begin to seek to understand. All that she knew was that she had dreamed her whole former life of flying and that now she felt as if she could. Dance and soaring, shout and song, and other celebratory voice and movement were all effortless in her resurrected body, when they had all been halting labor in her former state. The odd thing was, though, that she took little or no independent satisfaction in her resurrected powers. She didn't dance for the pleasure of dancing or soar for the pleasure of flight, although God would likely not have begrudged her any such pleasure. Her whole satisfaction was instead in being now in the full presence of God. She danced and soared to please him, showing to him her intense gratitude that to gain her a resurrected body in his own presence, he had offered her his own Son.

Truth

"'I am the truth.'" John 16:6.

PRAYER

We thank you, Father, for truth. We thank you for reality, for making a world in which things are as they are and that we can know them so to be. You made the world authentic, concrete, and genuine. You also made us to discern and know what is real. Indeed, you made us to report truth, to confirm for ourselves and relate to others when the premises that we form and constructs that we hold equate to what is real. You made reality inescapable, pressing its truths in upon us. You then made our description of reality necessary, forcing us to encounter it and make use of it to survive. You then brought your Son into this world that you have us encounter and use. You gave us your Son so that we could know not just reality but truth itself, reality lying within you who make all that is real. We dream only fantasies and fictions, while you speak and create the real. We thus find truth in your words, not in our own words, which are true only to the extent that your words measure them so. Without truth, waves of fantasy would swamp our unmoored boats, making sound and hopeful living impossible for us. With truth, your truth, Father, we live not just in hope but joyfully anticipating glory. Thank you, Father, for making the real, bringing us to the point of knowing it, and then giving us truth incarnate in your Son. Thank you for reality, authenticity, and the genuine. Thank you that we do not live in a world that we alone construct, each to his own imaginings.

ANSWER

I am not an imaginary god. I exist, and what I create is real. You are real, and so are your fellow persons and the world that you all encounter. You have not imagined yourselves into being, and your imagination doesn't change who, where, or what you are. Know the authenticity, order, and design of my world, and you will know more of me. You know me through my creation. You also know me through my Son and the Spirit whom I sent you after his ascension. My Son and Spirit are also real, as authentic and genuine as I am. My Son was in the world, just as my Spirit is now your guide and comforter in the world. I send my Spirit where I wish, my Spirit carrying my words and the image of my Son to you. Treat my Spirit as real as you treat my world, the world that you see all around you. You can touch the world that I created, but my Spirit touches you. Know the presence and touch of my Spirit, and you will know that I, too, am as real as the world you see and feel around you. My kingdom is also real. I have a kingdom that is as real as the world that you see and feel around you. My kingdom is in you and all around you. And because you know me and my creation to be real, my Son will draw you into my kingdom where you will see real things that you have not yet even imagined. You will join the resurrected in my kingdom as long as you know that I exist and that I reward those who eagerly seek me. Do not imagine the world other than as I present it to you. My word became flesh and walked among you to prove that I am the one true God who created you and the world, and who loves you.

TRANSFORMATION

He needed spiritual things to be real. Some, he knew, accepted that spiritual things might only be florid imagining and didn't care whether the spiritual was instead real. To some, imaginings, even fantasies, had the same value as the real. If they could imagine things, then they felt that they had the same meaning to them as did the real. Truth was unimportant, itself an imagining. If one could dream it, then the dream was in effect real. That was not how he thought, though. He needed to know truth, not imagining. He wanted what he believed about the world, including anything supernatural in, above, or about the world, to be genuine, testable, historical, reliable, and reproducible. He didn't want to act as if he and everyone else in the world imagined their own god. He didn't think that living that way would do anyone any good, least of all his family and himself. He had seen far too much harm come from pure imagining. He respected dreamers only to a point and not beyond where they pretended that their dreams were real or as good as real. This all was why he trusted the one great God whose Son came into the world. He knew that he could trust, indeed had by examination to accept, the historical event of the Son's coming. No one else had predicted his own demise and resurrection. In that respect, when the subject came to spirituality, he knew what was real and what was imagining. He would go with the real, thanking God for it.

REVELATION

He could quickly tell that the kingdom was no fantasy or illusion, even if its perfection gave it an unreal allure. He wasn't imagining heaven. He could feel that the kingdom was real. He knew the fantasy of dreams, having been a frequent dreamer. He knew both the terror and the appeal of dreams, knew that they were only deep-sleep imaginings. He had woken from every dream knowing that the dream had been unreal. By contrast, he knew from the start that he wasn't going to wake from kingdom slumber. He was fully alert and in control of all of his senses, not deaf, mute, or helpless as he had often been in dreams. His actions in dreams, in those few dreams where he was able to think and act, had little control over his weird dream environments that seemed to change unpredictably throughout the dream. By contrast, the kingdom environment was stable and largely predictable even if filled with wonders. Like earth, the kingdom had an order that the kingdom would not distort, alter, or deny. God was real, and his creations, both earth and kingdom, were also real. Just as God could not deny himself, so, too, would the kingdom not suddenly change its laws and order. He couldn't make sense of everything that he saw in the kingdom, just as he hadn't made sense of everything on earth. Yet he surely wasn't dreaming that he was in the kingdom. Indeed, the kingdom's stability and solidity, and the clarity with which he comprehended and interacted with it, made earth look just a little unreal. The kingdom constantly reminded him of Jesus declaring that he was truth. He now lived where Jesus lived meaning that all was especially authentic and stable, all especially material, physical, and real.

Rest

"'Come to me, and I will give you rest.'" Matthew 11:28.

PRAYER

We thank you, Father, for rest. Indeed, we thank you not merely for physical relaxation and recovery. We thank you further for giving us in you a place where our otherwise ceaseless yearnings abate. Nothing satisfies us but you, even though we continually crave satisfaction apart from you. We cannot get enough of pleasure, purpose, or pride, indeed of any of the things with which we try to quell our human hunger and quench our spiritual thirst. You alone give us our fiery desire's quenching drink. When we turn away from you to try to find our peace, we find only brief reprieve in things that we know will soon destroy us if we continue their vain pursuit. They hold only momentary relief for us, and even that a false hope. We need instead to turn to you for godly contentment, that which we know from experience is great gain. In your embrace, our barren deserts become your grassy fields, our hot winds your cool breeze, and our scorching sun your cool shade. One day in your court refreshes us for a thousand days elsewhere. We remember those days in your presence, Father, and thank you for them, for in them you have given us eternal peace, contentment, satisfaction, and rest. We thank you for that rest, without which we would be unbearable beings. You give us the peace that withstands all burdens. You give us complete and eternal rest.

Answer

You should indeed turn to me for rest. I hold your peace. I hold your contentment. Your busy days wear you out. You find no conclusion to them. You cannot make sufficient order out of the many things that you herd and chase. They do not produce what you expect and so do not satisfy you. Everything for you is chasing after the wind, until you turn toward me. Then I can once again be your peace and solace. I can once again restore you with my rest. You can then regain your equilibrium and equanimity, recover your bloom and balance. You find peace in me because I am your creator. I designed you to rest in me. I made your mind to dwell on me, your voice to speak my word, and your body to pursue and worship me. Only I am great enough to fill the void that you sense in you. That void I made for me. Your mind fevers to know me. Your will yearns to pursue my path. Your ears itch to hear accounts of my glory. Your eyes strain to see me act. Your belly will always be hungry, and your mouth will always thirst. What you eat and drink never lasts. Yet the food and drink that I give you, indeed the flesh and blood of my own Son, grants you peace and contentment eternally. And because you have thanked me for that peace that surpasses all understanding, I will make you lie down in such verdant green pastures that you will never be anxious to leave.

Transformation

She one day suddenly realized that she sought a peace that she had never quite grasped. Her life had felt too much like the lives of so many of her acquaintances around her. They seemed always a good bit harried and too much harassed. They never quite stopped moving, never quite relaxed. They flitted from one thing to another, never quite finishing any thought or task. She too often had the same sense that her life was simply aimless motion. Oh, she had her purposes, and she hoped that they were also God's purposes. Yet the way in which she went about her day didn't quite give her the peace that those purposes should have given her. She didn't quite find contentment in the tasks even when they were godly tasks. She finally began to consider why she sensed ill at ease about her nearly frantic motion, her inability to seem at all at ease. Gradually, she came to the conclusion that her contentment wasn't in God's will or task, not in the godly service or suffering. Rather, her contentment was in him alone. Indeed, she could have stood silently by at the temple all her life waiting for a glimpse of him, with that singular focus, and been content all of her life. She needn't mow the green pastures that God had made for her. She could rest in him. He would do the rest.

Revelation

In the kingdom, she finally found her rest. She still took great joy in discovering God's rich kingdom embellishments, those wonders that celebrated the glory of God. She felt that God wanted her to make those discoveries so that she had continual fresh cause to celebrate him. Yet she also for the first time found true rest in him. The restlessness of her former life was past. In the kingdom, she could stop her ceaseless movement. She could simply dwell in respite in him. On occasion after occasion, she would find that she had stopped so completely in him and stayed still in him for so long that she could not measure how much time had passed. She suspected that time stood still whenever she stopped to rest in him. How this rest occurred remained a mystery to her. Because he was always accessible to her, and also always present, she could literally just stop moving and still her mind, and feel as if he had completely surrounded her. Sometimes, she would find a quiet place to sit, other times a special vista over which to gaze, and other times a green pasture in which to lay down. Her posture, though, really didn't matter. Whenever she wished, which was very often, almost seeming to be continuously, she could just relax into him. He then seemed to hold her, perhaps to cuddle her as a gentle giant might cuddle and protect a beloved plaything. Nothing interrupted these frequent occasions, certainly no alarm but also not even any call to activity or chores. In these frequent times, nothing seemed to go undone. In God's rest, she never shirked duties or otherwise fell behind. God's rest wasn't at all like acting lazy, like failing to show sufficient industry. He gave her full permission simply to dwell quietly at peace with him for as long and as often as she wished, which was in fact long and often. Whatever was the kingdom operation of this wonderful thing, she simply had rest like she always wished but never experienced on earth. God constantly refreshed her as she rested in him.

4

Supplication

"Hear the supplications of your servant." 2 Chronicles 6:21.

Father, you know that we have many requests of you. You have heard our adoration, confession, and thanksgiving. We now come to you with those many requests. We know that you will answer all that we ask that lies within your will for us. We know that our asking you makes a difference in what you do. We know that you want us to ask and that for asking you reward us with answers that we would not have had without asking. Indeed, we know that our asking causes you to shower down ever more richly all that you have for us. You are the God whose love and generosity exceeded all bounds in your Son's sacrifice. We appreciate that you have for us material things to sustain us, for which you only wanted us to ask. We also appreciate that you sometimes have for us labors, good works through which you will provide for others if we would only ask. We know, too, that other times you have for us rest from labor, the relief and restoration that we often need if we would only ask you for it. You even have for us old fellowship and new friendship, and at other times solitude and peace, if we would only ask. Our requests and your answers help us discover new capacity, bring us new insight, and give us new character, if we would only ask. You would both bring justice and then show mercy, if we would only ask. You would bring us the sick for you to heal, hungry for you to feed, homeless for you to shelter, and lost souls for you to save, all if we would only ask. Hear our prayers, Father, for we have so much to ask and so much more to receive from you.

Provision

"I will bless with abundant provision." Psalm 132:15.

PRAYER

Father, we first ask that you would provide for us. We ask that you provide for our needs. Please give to us those things that will sustain us, whether food, clothing, shelter, or other necessity. You know our needs and have always met them. Why should you not do so now, when you know and we confess that we have equal or greater need of you? As our Father, you are first and last to provide, the only one who can meet all of our needs, especially when our critical need is for you. No one can offer us you, other than your Son whom you sent for us. Continue to so provide for us, Father, both because we ask and because providing for us is so plainly within your gracious will. Then further provide not just for our need but to satisfy our righteous desires, especially when those desires are only for more of you. We desire more of your grace, more of your presence, more of your purpose and power, more of knowing your will. We desire more knowledge of you. We want to see more of you in the image, words, and actions of your Son, so that we would honor and pursue more of you. We desire more of your Holy Spirit who would help us to see and know more of you. Yes, Father, provide for us abundantly, especially when that provision is you.

ANSWER

You should indeed ask me whenever you have needs or desires. You are right to look to me for provision. I am your constant provider, and not only when all else fails. My provision is most generous, so far beyond what anyone or anything else can provide you that have no reason to look anywhere else for your provision. Others will tempt you to believe that you depend on them, when instead you truly depend only on me. The reasons for which you ask are nonetheless important to me. You know my desire that you know and glorify me through my Son. I do not give my glory to others. Let your purpose in asking be to trust and rely on me for my glory and the glory of my Son. Then I will answer richly indeed, out of the riches of my glory. Your needs and desires I will fill until you overflow with your own love and generosity, their source being in my love and generosity. I answer every one of your requests when you ask with the right motives. I do not answer requests that you or others make when asked with the wrong motives. I am your thinking and judging God, with my Spirit as your guide and conscience. I do not contradict my own will with my own actions. I desire your provision in order that I have your love and devotion, which is in itself your provision. When you love and desire me, I come to you and make you whole. I cannot provide for you otherwise. To give you things that remove you from me is not to provide for you. And because you have asked for provision with the right motives, I have granted your request. You will live abundantly in my Spirit, with my answer having provided richly in all good things for you.

TRANSFORMATION

She could not quite see *how* God had provided so abundantly for her, although she could see that he clearly *had* so provided. While she faced challenges like the challenges others faced, she seldom or never felt that she lacked the provisions to meet them. God always brought her through with all that she had needed to face and survive every challenge. He somehow even helped her prosper through them. God's provision wasn't for her to avoid the pitfalls of her ordinarily complex life, just as ordinary and complex as anyone else's day-to-day life. She also didn't manage to navigate her challenges with any special alacrity. God's provision didn't make her superior to others. Just as she faced daily pitfalls not of her own making, she also had just about as many pratfalls of her own making as did others. God's provision for her was instead to see that she had all that she needed in him to manage getting through those daily challenges and complexities, while maintaining the faith with which he had imbued her. He was giving her all that she needed to continue to love and adore him, indeed to grow in love and devotion. In so discerning, she realized for the first time that his primary provision wasn't the material things that she managed to acquire for her day-to-day survival. His primary provision for her was the faith to continue to look to him, see more of him, and grow more in her devotion to him. After all, if she gained the whole world but lost him, then she would have nothing. Realizing as much, she decided to pray more often and earnestly that he provide more richly for her, not that she might have greater ease or pleasure, but solely in order that she grow in devotion.

REVELATION

The kingdom provided abundantly, she could tell from her first exploration. God had made the place a paradise. The kingdom met her every need. She never hungered and never thirsted. She was never cold or hot other than as she desired. She never lacked shelter nor rest. She always had company when she wished and solitude when she desired. Her healing was instant whenever she needed it. She always had energy and always had strength. She never lacked courage for whatever adventure that the kingdom offered. In all that the kingdom provided, she hadn't truly to ask God. He was instead always present, aware of her need, and already supplying the generous good to meet it. She had imagined the kingdom as simply bountiful, as if God had set a great table for her enjoyment and the enjoyment of others, and then stepped back to watch them partake of its bounty. Yet the kingdom wasn't God absent but instead God present. She sensed as her needs arose and the kingdom satisfied them that God was continually setting and resetting the table, indeed making the table just for her as she desired it. She also sensed that in doing so, he was acting as both servant and King, just as Christ had done in gaining her entry into the kingdom. She received his service gratefully while honoring him solely as King. He was meeting her every need not so that she could revel in pleasure but so that she could revel in him, witnessing his glory. The kingdom's bounty gave her constant opportunity to witness and worship him.

Shelter

"Dwell in the Most High's shelter; rest in the Almighty's shadow." Psalm 91:1.

PRAYER

Oh, Father, how badly we need your shelter. Yes, we need the shelter of a roof over our heads, giving us warmth against winter, dry against rains, and cool against the summer sun. We ask for safe and secure physical shelter. We also ask that you would provide shelter for those who are near to losing it and also for the homeless who have already suffered that loss. We are not alone in our needs for shelter. Help us also to see the need that others have for shelter and to respond to that need where you give us the means. Help us, in other words, to invite into our own homes the homeless stranger. Turn our hearts and efforts toward giving others your shelter. Yet beyond the physical security of which we all have need, we ask that you supply us with the shelter, comfort, and security of your Holy Spirit. Extend your gentle wing over us, creating for us a spiritual habitation where we feel your warmth against isolation's cold and your cool against anger's heat. Give our minds your comforting accommodation, banishing our anxious and frightful thoughts. Hide us in your sacred tent against the marauding bands who would steal our souls. Let the storms of trials, strife, and emotion pass quickly, with your sheltering wisdom preserving our faith. Let us wander no more, having found and taken your shelter. Shelter us even from your own judgment, hiding us under your Son's precious blood, that we may take shelter in your righteous presence.

ANSWER

Yes, I will grant you shelter that you may live in faith. You will live secure from the elements and predators, not alone for your comfort, but in order that you may boldly share eternal life through my Son. I grant you temporal shelter when I send you my Spirit, while I granted you eternal shelter when I sent you my Son. I give shelter generously, but also sometimes deny shelter as I did for a time to Nebuchadnezzar, in order that you may exhibit faith. I do not want you hungry, and I do not want you cold. I do not want your enemies to have access to you, nor do I want you exposed. When you hear the wind whip outside your home, and when you see the temperature plunge or soar, then think of me sheltering you. Think of my love for you and how I want you loving me. I hold your home. I am your mansion, the glorious one with whom my Son prepares a room for you. You have my promise that you will always have such a room. When your earthly shelter crumbles, you will flee to me, with whom you will find your eternal home. Your eternal home with me will be unlike any earthly abode in that you will never fear its loss, never question its security, never doubt its comfort. And because you have also asked for shelter for others in addition to yourself, I will grant you the will, time, and means to help them also to find my shelter. You will introduce them to my Son so that they, too, will find their eternal home.

TRANSFORMATION

He loved his earthly home only as much as he perceived in it the Spirit of his coming eternal dwelling. He hadn't taken much stock in homes as he grew up. His family of origin had moved often and lived in many homes, altering each to their needs and for their comfort. Some homes had been tiny and rough, while others had been spacious. Some were secure against natural depredations in varying degrees, while others were not. Most were secure against human depredation. None of those homes, though, had given him the shelter of his Lord, at least not that he could reckon. His origin family had not spoken of Christ or honored Jesus in them. God's word was not in those homes, not in the hearts and minds, and not on the tongues, of the people who resided in them. And so the homes for the most part kept out the literal wind but less so the figurative storms. Physical provision was not the issue, as each family member found enough for his or her own keep. Faith and spiritual security, though, were significant issues. Each family member pursued his or her own god, all of them idols. The pursuit left the family and its individual members in peril, chastened and weakened. When by contrast he started his own family with a wife of faith, God gave their home his sheltering Spirit. God provided for them just as they had asked. They had asked for shelter to invite God into their home, and God had granted their request richly. He, his wife, and their child lived long and happily in the home, comforted and guided by God's Spirit.

REVELATION

He found the kingdom's shelter to be exactly as he had hoped in its primary effect. Everywhere he rested, everywhere he paused, in any place that he even momentarily called his home or abode, he had the presence of God. No lodging of any kind was without the loving Lord's presence. He often took respite in convenient little places, sometimes small depressions in an open windy dune, other times in a shady sylvan glade or a boulder's sheltering outcrop. None of these places had the improvements of a shelter no less of a home. They didn't have roof or wall, bench or bed. Although these places were only waystations and he was at those times seemingly alone, the Lord was nonetheless always present. He could see the Lord's smile, hear the Lord's greeting, and feel the Lord's gentle breath on his face or neck. From these reassuring moments, he quickly realized that his shelter was not in the place or its appointments but rather in the presence of the Lord. The places where he paused in his journeys, even if still in God's paradise, were often materially inhospitable in that they held no particular physical comfort and even little protection. They were often bare and exposed. Yet with the good Lord present, they were always home, always a secure and resting abode. Because the Lord accompanied him, he could have lingered long in any one of those places. He could have made any waystation his permanent home. They all had the one thing that he most needed, which was the shelter that the Lord's presence provided. He was always at peace, always secure, always restful, and always sheltered because always with the Lord. The kingdom had given him the shelter for which he had long asked. He would always have his home with the Lord.

Protection

"He gives us a wall of protection." Ezra 9:9.

PRAYER

Father, we ask and need not just your shelter but also your protection. We can take shelter in you, in your house, indeed under your wing. Yet then beyond our accommodation, we need your defense and fortification. We find ourselves under constant attack with moods, attitudes, and enemies sapping our energy and spirit. We cannot see your light for the smoke of battle all around us. War wages for our souls. Battles ensue over our spirits. Disease, disability, dismemberment, and death threaten us daily, yes, but more than mortal threats, we face spiritual brawls, combat for our passions, personalities, and souls. You, though, guard, shield, and secure us. You guard us first against physical menace and then against moral hazard, against the sin that would steal our hearts and claim our souls. We need this protection from you, oh Father. We need safety that only your Holy Spirit can provide. Send your Spirit swiftly and surely to guard our hearts and minds. Gather your angels about us, raising shield and spear against attackers on all sides. Prove yourself able again on our behalf. You have no enemy who threatens you. Every enemy perishes at your command. Act as our sentinel and guard, Father, for we are in dire need of your protection. Protect here your people.

ANSWER

Just as I give you shelter, I also protect you when you venture forth on my mission. I am your advance scout and your rearguard. I warn you of approaching dangers and keep enemies from your back. I am on your right and left flanks, armed to protect you. You may carry word of my Son far and wide without fear of destruction. Only when you abandon my mission in pursuit of your own corrupt designs need you fear destruction. Then, your fierce enemies will overtake you. They who have no claim or power over me will nonetheless be your destruction, with my protection withdrawn. I do not favor your tormentors. Indeed, they will face their own destruction. Yet I will not protect you against your own corrupt designs. Your tyrants and bullies are not your protectors, but they can serve as reminder of your need for my protection. Your protection depends on your devotion to me. Why would I protect those who have no regard for me? Let their own manipulations be their own weak protectors. I who am stronger than all others protect those who love and follow me. I protect those who carry word of my Son with them to share with others, that all may join in glorifying me. And because you have prayed with right motives for my protection, I will safeguard you against all your enemies in order that you will be mine.

TRANSFORMATION

She knew something about spiritual battles. She had seen them waged in others and could sense them waged in herself. They had at one time buffeted her in ways that showed her the possibility of her demise. Yet as her years stretched into decades of relying on the Lord, the possibility of her demise receded into impossibility. She knew with ever greater confidence that she had the Lord's protection. She had long known that the Lord had the power to protect. Only in her later years did she trust that she was within his protection. Her confidence was not in her own righteousness. Instead, she sensed that her increasing devotion to her Savior had something to do with her confidence. Her confidence was instead in her Savior, about whom the Spirit was teaching her ever more. The more that she learned of her Savior, the more that she trusted in his salvation, and the more that she sensed the Lord's protection. Her witness to others bolstering their faith accelerated her sense that the Lord would never let her go, would never give her over to her enemies. As she lived more for Jesus and less for herself, she lived with greater awareness that she needed and received the Lord's protection. She saw more of the great temptations and corruptions that threatened her, while she simultaneously sensed less of any fear of them. She could see her enemies more clearly than ever and yet knew that she was in the care of the Lord. God had always held her in his hand. Now, though, he had also let her know that he had answered her frightened prayers for protection.

REVELATION

The kingdom protected her so completely that until then she had not thought such protection possible. She knew that she had been frequently under attack in her former place. Illnesses, accidents, confusion, depression, disagreements, division, and struggles had arisen one after the other. Attacks of various kinds had been so common that she had hardly realized just how under siege she had felt. Her siege mentality became so constant and normal that she hardly noticed its weight, although she could see its debilitating effect on her health and emotions, her relationships and responsibilities, and on the people around her. When she prayed for protection, she usually prayed for the protection of others, when she ought also to have prayed for her own protection. The attacks that she fought and resisted were that common and devious. She had periodic victories in those battles, every one of them hard won. She also had losses when she would let briefly go of her Lord and lose her sense of his strength and faith. The kingdom, though, was not a place of battle. In the kingdom, the Lord ruled without protest or dissent. Not only had the Lord won the war, but he had also extinguished the last battles. No enemy infiltrated the kingdom. His protection was thus complete. All attack, sin, and corruption ended at the kingdom's unassailable gate. She was utterly safe in the kingdom, free not just from loss but also from attack. God had answered her own prayer for protection, even if she had prayed primarily for others. The kingdom had taught her the full value of God as her protector. Her full kingdom relief, he had long ago won.

Communication

"He explained to them what the scriptures said about himself." Luke 24:27.

PRAYER

Father, we ask that you would speak to us. Communicate with us, letting us know your thoughts, desires, and will. Hear us, and register our prayers, but then react and respond in ways that we can perceive and understand. When you speak, please do not judge us, for we are under the blood of your Son. Speak instead in your generous grace and great mercy. Let us know that you hear our prayers, whether we pray in adoration, confession, thanks, or request. Then let us know that you are answering. We ask that you converse and commune with us, Father, as we know that you do, but now making your conversation evident. If we are not fit in our own communication with you, then help us properly to converse and commune with you. Your thoughts are so far above our thoughts. Yet you must make them known to us in our ways, not alone in your ways. Give us signs and wonders, yes, but above all give us your word, that precious communication from you whose word authors our life. Father, speak with us that we may know that you hear our prayers of adoration. We want only to glorify you. But to do so, we must know that we speak to you just as you desire. Walk and talk with us in the way that your Son tread the Emmaus road. Reveal yourself to us that we may speak of you and to you as you would have us do. While we need your guidance, warning, admonition, and approbation, we above all need your simple communication. Father, we need to hear and know you.

ANSWER

You have my word, indeed my living Word in the image and Spirit of my Son, to reassure you that I listen and respond to you. I communicate with you through my word and my Spirit who lives within you. My actions that you perceive through the people with whom, and circumstances with which, I surround you also speak to you. My responses come to you in many forms, from my Spirit's gentle whisper, to my words that your mind recalls, and through what happens in and around you. You can recognize my many responses in that my responses are always consistent with my word. When you see my word revealed around you and within you, you know that I am responding. I communicate often and freely with you. I am not your obstacle. Your blindness and deafness are your obstacles. Look up to me, and listen for me. I am always speaking to you and with you. My Spirit is your constant companion, living within you, just as you reside within my Spirit. I welcome that you beseech my communication, but you have no need to wonder or doubt that I speak. Do not let your lack of faith in me be your obstacle. See how I respond, and hear how I speak. My word is all around you and in you. Turn to me, and listen to me. Listen to those whom I send you. You can tell whom I send when their words reflect my word. You will hear my word if you listen. My communication indeed blesses you when you listen to me.

TRANSFORMATION

That God would speak with humans meant everything to him. For a reason that he did not know, words had always meant a lot to him. He read constantly and wrote often. He had listened much while speaking little in his earlier life, and now he spoke much but also listened much. Indeed, he had discovered by mid-life that God had intended him for communication. God had made him to listen, hear, understand, and discern. God had also made him to communicate including to speak but more so to write. He hadn't for a long time understood why God had called him to a ministry of communication, until God had prepared him sufficiently to hear, think, discern, and write. What God had done more than anything else, though, in his preparation for communication, was to show him how to hear what God spoke. God wanted him first to recognize what God was saying to him for himself and others, and then to speak and write those words. He was to share God's word in speaking and writing, as other followers were to share God's word in the unique ways that he called each of them. Although he had very far yet to go, he had learned to hear God communicate. God was speaking all around him.

Revelation

He had wondered how God would communicate in the kingdom, certainly hoping and expecting that God often would. On earth, he had read God's word repeatedly for the satisfaction of God's communication. In scripture, God spoke in ways that he could hear and comprehend. He listened also to sermons, messages, and songs, through which he also sensed that God spoke. Prayer had been less fruitful for him, too often leaving him with the sense only of having talked rather than also listened, perhaps because he had seldom prayed that God would speak. Meditation gave him glimpses of God's thoughts. He also saw rare signs and symbols from which he drew tentative meaning as to God's intent. In all, he hoped that the kingdom would supply him with God's abundant communication rather than leaving him looking at signs and symbols as God's cypher. The kingdom, of course, did not disappoint. God's voice was everywhere, both expressed and implicit, audible and in sign. He could hear God's voice both in words and in the wind, waves, or babbling brook. Indeed, everyone spoke the word of God. God's kingdom communication was clearer not because he spoke louder or more often but because no one heard any other words. Every word was a word and message from the Lord, no matter who spoke or when spoken. The kingdom permitted no frivolous words, no unholy talk. Of communication the kingdom had plenty, but it was all God talk. He found his relief profound. He had not realized how godless chatter, both his own and that of others, had drained his former life. The kingdom sustained him on God's word, just as the word had always been with

God, been God, and been the author of life. God had answered his desire for communication.

Justice

"Let justice roll on like a river." Amos 5:24.

PRAYER

Father, we petition you that you would give us justice in our struggles against adversaries. We have adversaries who mislead and oppose us, who distract, damage, and degrade us, without cause that we can discern. We face enemies who should be friends, opponents who should be allies, and burdens where we should find benefactors. We have adversaries both seen and unseen. They darken our minds so that we can hardly see your light. They weigh us down so that we can hardly move on your behalf. Give us your advocate, Father, your defender and protector to seek justice on our behalf. Avenge both our visible and unseen offenders. Then provide us with justice's appropriate relief. Reset the boundary stone where it first stood. Restore the reputation of the righteous. Protect our rights and lands. Equip for us counselors who stand at the ready to draw up righteous demands. Help them make holy petitions on our behalf. Give us defenders who have access to your courts and who know how and for whom you will rightly judge. Even as you give to our enemies your righteous judgment, also give us courage to advocate the just interests of the vulnerable and oppressed. Turn your back on the oppressor. Reward the righteous who honor your covenants. Reward the holy for their noble duties fulfilled. Give us justice against those who oppress us, Father, for we are in dire need of your just relief. We need your justice even while we hold fast to the mercy that you promise us in our trust in your Son.

ANSWER

You are right to turn to me for justice because only I hold all things true. I am he who determines right from wrong. I am the tree of the knowledge of good and evil. Those who hold true to me discern justice. Those who reject me offend. Only I can provide you the just relief that you seek. You will not find adequate recourse from any other source. Your bargains and compromises with your offenders will give you no relief. You will fall further into their clutches with every effort to extricate yourself without my assist. Leave your enemies and reprobates to me. I will do them justice. Do not take my justice into your own hands. Do not exact your own punishment lest you also offend. Do not give your offender a cause against you. Then I would have to turn my just wrath on you as much as on your offender. Keep your hands clean of another's blood. Hold fast to my Son for your true course, while I alone avenge for you. Everyone receives their due from me, whether punishment or reward. When you hold fast to my Son, you receive your due, which is eternal reward. When others ignore my Son while continuing in their offenses, they receive their due, which is banishment from me, as my just punishment. No one should want justice from me who does not hold first and fast to my Son. And because you ask for my justice in the name and under the blood of my Son, I grant your request. You will receive your just reward, while your enemies I will punish.

TRANSFORMATION

She needed justice, her Lord's swift and sure justice. The offense that she had just endured, and from which she suspected that she would now take long to recover, was greater than any she had anticipated. From any lesser offense, she was sure that she could have turned the other cheek. This offense, though, had unfairly exposed and unduly shamed her in so many ways. It had wrongly harmed her reputation and relationships, undermined her position and trust, and caused wounds that would long affect her, likely in ways that she would labor hard to discover and remedy. The offense's greatest challenge, though, was that she had no way of her own out of it. No disclosure or recourse that she could imagine or muster would give her any relief. Impossible consequences hemmed her in, in every direction that she turned. Over and over, she could feel her frustration feeding the anger welling within her. Each time, she would press it back down. Then she remembered that the Lord would avenge the wrong that she suffered. She decided to write down each specific aspect of the wrong. She then committed each wrong, one by one, to the Lord's swift and sure justice. Even as she did so, she felt glimmers of relief that she hoped in time would turn into the torrents that she needed to cleanse her of this wrong. She didn't want her tormentor to cause her to stumble, to turn a tormentor's sin into a victim's wrong.

REVELATION

As she had fully expected, the kingdom was entirely fair and just. The kingdom's gates, and the cleansing that Jesus had made of everyone who passed through them, ensured the banishment of every predilection to injustice. Under God's unquestioned rule, residents treated one another exactly as they should. Residents in their thorough obedience to God's perfect order simply avoided disputes long before they had sown and germinated. Equity reigned. None sought advantage over others. What she hadn't expected, though, is how significant was the difference that the kingdom's complete justice made for its residents. Until she grew accustomed to kingdom life enough to look back with perspective on her former life, she hadn't realized how heavily injustice burdened that former life. In retrospect, nearly everything in her former life seemed unjust. She could see in every memory that she had both advantage and disadvantage that she did not deserve, that her actions and intentions had not warranted. She had won when she should have lost but also lost when she should have won. She had privilege and ease where she had earned none but then hindrance and difficulty where she should have had privilege and ease. She committed offenses both when intending and not intending them, and without cause to offend, while she suffered offenses both intended and unintended, and undeserved. Her days had seemed to stumble from one difficult situation into another, always with the claims and causes confused, and never with the full satisfaction of just result. The kingdom resolved and eliminated completely her former life's morass of injustices. She felt as if Christ had washed her clean of one great mess, largely of her own making, which of course he had. He had answered her prayer fully and finally. She had full justice because she had his salvation and had him.

Healing

"I will heal my people." Jeremiah 33:6.

PRAYER

Father, we once again need your healing. How often have we ailed, how often have we suffered, how often have we turned to you to heal? You know our constant need, which is that you repair again this corrupted flesh. We so look forward to that day when you will transform these weak vessels in which we struggle, into glorious bodies in which we will rejoice for eternity. Until then, Father, we need you once again to set these bodies aright, whether by your own miracle word or in guiding the skilled hand of the surgeon and sure care of the nurse. Restore circulation and function, repair system and limb. Ease pain, calm the anxious mind, and then help us to walk, laugh, and run, and above all to worship you again. Help us to lift our voices and arms in praise of your healing hand. Help us to dance before you in your honor and to play the instrument with skill in your salute. Heal us that we may again lead the parade that hails you. Oh Father, we have more honor to give you, more of the good works that you planned for us to do, more service to bestow on the needful, and more of your Son's salvation to share with the lost. We only need your healing to do so. Do not leave us bereft of the means to carry out your will. Make us strong again for your good purpose. Heal our scars into tissue stronger than before the wound. Make every sickness from which we recover produce in us greater-than-ever capacity to perform as you will. And as you heal us, show us what you do so that we may testify to your curative wonders. Heal us, Father, that even in our healing we may glorify you.

ANSWER

I am your healer and physician. As your maker, I design and direct your body's course. You are right to ask me for healing. Because I created you, I am able to recreate you, to restore your body at my will. I knit you together in the womb, and so I know how to make you anew, restoring your strength, beauty, and function. Your body may fail even to the point of death, but I can raise you from the dead. If I can raise you from the dead, then I can also heal any condition less than death. I can heal you on my own or through the hands of a skilled physician. I can heal you on my own or through the prayers of one who prays in the name of Christ. Your healing may be swift or slow, complete or partial, as I choose it. You play a role in your own healing when you listen to me and those whom I send to heal you. Your body is my temple. Do not despair of me when your healing is not what you expected. While I desire to heal, and I grant healing prayer far more often than those who pray for healing realize it, trust me in how slow or fast, complete or partial is your healing. Everything that I do is for your good. I also desire above all that you join me in eternity. No one in a corrupted world lives naturally forever. When I choose not to allow you to remain trapped in your natural body on earth, I do so in order that you may join me in your glorified body in eternity. In your resurrection, I will transform your body so that it does not corrupt. Your transformed body will inflict no more pain or suffering. I heal, and I deliver. And so because you have asked for healing, I will heal you more generously and surely than you thought possible or could imagine. Watch for my healing glory.

TRANSFORMATION

He had both seen and experienced miraculous healing, although he suspected that he did not fully know how glorious and generous God was as a healer. He considered for the first time that under God's gently healing hand, he had probably recovered from mortal illnesses the symptoms of which he had not yet even felt. He realized that God had likely silently corrected conditions that were just about to debilitate or kill him. He also suspected for the first time that under God's protective hand, he had miraculously avoided maladies and injuries about which he at the time did not even know. God must have been constantly healing him and those whom he loved, often without any evidence of the need for healing. He had on the other hand long known that God was constantly healing through skilled care providers. He and his family had under medical care so often had prompt recoveries from painful disorders, so quickly, that they had nearly forgotten how serious were the conditions. He had also healed from debilitating conditions without medical care, under God's hand alone. Yet what he now appreciated most about God as a healer was the silent way in which God must go about regulating, repairing, and restoring bodily functions even before one's mind had realized the grave threat of undisclosed conditions. He didn't want to think again of God as a reluctant healer. He was going to praise God for his constant care, just as much as for the miraculous healing.

REVELATION

The kingdom healed like miracle balm, except that the miracle was not ointment but instead the loving hand of God. He could feel God's restorative power as if it were God's very hand, as perhaps it was. God had knit him together in the womb, and so he was sure that God could make him new in heaven. His resurrected body bore his own prior image. Anyone who knew him in his former life would also have recognized him in the kingdom. Yet in entering the kingdom, he had somehow left behind every broken bit of his tired old form. God had healed every pore of the body he now wore in the kingdom. He had on earth prayed so often for healing, sometime his own though far more often the healing of others. He could then have concluded that God did not always heal those for whom he had prayed. Not all of them, at least, had an earthly recovery. He had not, though, thought of healing as an eternal rather than temporal question. God did heal all those whom he welcomed into heaven, every one of them with entire rather than only partial healing. While resurrected bodies could bear earth's identifiers, as Christ himself had borne his crucifixion's marks, every resurrected body still had complete function, ability, and relief. Every resurrected body had complete healing. God was not a halfway deity but an all-the-way God of generous healing. He thus had not a single ache nor pain in heaven, when his earthly body had formerly ached and pained him much. The kingdom had freed him from the distraction of those pains, giving him all the restored freedom and function to worship his healing God. God wished his eternity to be free for him to do that for which God had made him.

Heart

"The Lord seeks out one after his own heart." 1 Samuel 13:14.

PRAYER

Father, we pray that you would give us your heart. You once had an earthly king about whom you said he was after your own heart. Make us like that earthly king who pursued you. If we had your heart, both a heart for you and a heart like yours, then oh how relationships and conditions around us would change. Your heart would free us of so many corruptions. Your heart is so pure, powerful, and purposeful that it would transform all who pursue and embrace it. If we only had your heart, then love, healing, creativity, trust, and intimacy would abound. Your kingdom would have come to earth as your kingdom is in heaven. Father, we want the sum of our parts, that whole made up of our thoughts, emotions, spirit, attitude, and ambitions, to reflect the image of your glorious Son. We want each to take on our unique identity in the divine nature of your Son. We want a heart that would compel us to pursue your will and please you. Remove from us our natural self-seeking heart, under the influence of which we pursue our own pleasures. Replace our natural heart with a supernatural heart that discerns your Holy Spirit and seeks you. Make of our hearts an organ for your Holy Spirit in which your love, shown so gloriously in your sacrifice of your Son, communes. Father, we pray for a new heart, your heart, the only heart that endures, the only temperament fit for your eternal kingdom.

ANSWER

Because you have asked, you will indeed have my heart, although you are not empty now. You are not without my heart. My Spirit living within you brings you my heart. You no longer have your old heart of stone when you have my Spirit living within you. How will you know that you have my heart? When you have a heart for my Son, then you have my heart, because my heart is for my Son. My Son's heart was to do my will, which was to love and save you. My Son saved you, showing my heart for you. When my Son completed his work, I drew him back to my heart because my heart is for my Son and my heart is my Son. When I drew my Son back to my heart, I sent you the Spirit to bring you the heart of my Son. My Son gave up his life for you, as you must give up your old heart in order to receive the heart of my Son. You will know that you are giving up your old heart as your heart for my Son increases. I cannot send you my heart unless you have a heart for my Son. Anyone who rejects my Son, refusing to do as he said, will not receive my heart, because my Son spoke as I directed him. My Son said that you must give up your life to have the life that I offer you, as the only way to save your life. My Son was speaking of my heart for you, of my heart that you must receive in you. Those who hold onto their old life cannot receive my new heart, which is the only heart that will save them. And because you have sought my heart, I will give you not only my heart but also my mind to know the purpose that I have for you.

TRANSFORMATION

She could feel her Lord's heart within her. She was not always in tune with that heart. Indeed, she could often feel it most within her when she was not acting as the Lord's heart desired. Then, the Lord's heart seemed to cry out to her that she had abandoned her love for him in order to love herself or another. These times were always painful for her, even as she sensed the Lord's loss, too. She had a hard time knowing why she would turn from the Lord's heart in these times other than that she had not fully relinquished her old heart to him. Her old heart still had its small grip on her, leading her away from the Lord's heart. She hoped that in time, the Lord would show her where she still clung to her hold heart. That gentle revelation, she discerned, was what was going on when she sensed the Lord's broken heart crying out to her. He was showing her that she still gripped her old heart, the one that she needed to relinquish to him in order that his heart could fill her with the life that he offered her. She heard him reminding her that if she held onto her old heart, then she would perish in doing so, while when she took the Lord's heart, she would live forever. As these quiet but painful conversations continued deep within her, they slowly loosened her grip on her old heart, which turned her from her Lord less and less often. She wanted to keep reminding herself of this slow and painful process of giving her heart to the Lord, painful not as much for her as for the Lord each time that she turned from him. Her turning away from God, she remembered, was why Jesus suffered the agony of the cross. Painful indeed, she thought again, while loosening her old grip further in favor of her Lord's heart, as she contemplated the cross.

REVELATION

She felt quite as if the kingdom had given her a new heart. Her kingdom heart was so pure and reliable that she hardly recognized it. In her former life, she had felt in a continual tug of war with her old heart. Her old heart had so often deceived her, turning her desires from the Lord to things for which she had no true taste, things that she knew were only temporary diversions. Her old heart was all over the place, pushing and pulling her at once in several directions. She could hardly wake each day without wondering where her heart would that day take her. She had committed her soul to the Lord, and yet her heart seemed less than fully committed in the direction that she had chosen. Her heart had seemed beyond cure. Yet the kingdom cured it or gave her a new heart. Her kingdom heart had one love, the Lord whom her will and soul had chosen. Her kingdom heart always moved in the same direction, which was toward her Lord, just as she desired. Indeed, her heart often sensed the direction in which the Lord walked nearby, or the direction in which he leapt and ran ahead of her, before her senses could anticipate his presence and pursue his movement. Her kingdom heart was always for the Lord, like a compass always pointing to the North Star. She slowly learned that she could trust her kingdom heart to lead her forward in the Lord's will and direction. She loved the purity that her heart had for the Lord, loved that her heart was now an organ of his design and desire. Her kingdom heart's single devotion greatly simplified and amplified her kingdom life. She could see that she ought in her former life to have prayed more often and earnestly for a pure heart, the lovely and reliable kingdom heart that she now had, which was her Lord's heart. God had given her a new heart in his own time and for his own good purpose.

Families

"Every family derives its name from the Father." Ephesians 3:15.

PRAYER

We pray for families, Father, in their time of great need. The times stress and break our families. Our families are in crisis. They are as much threat as haven. They are as much burden as relief. They should provide support, stability, and rest but instead degrade and disrupt us. They distract us from you who are our Savior. Your family would show love and provide intimacy, but our families harbor conflict and strife. Your family would lift up, while ours break apart and tear down. Make safe harbors again of our families, Father. Give our families the footing that faith in you supplies. Make them rocks again on which to build shelter from storms. Help them to care, educate, and provide. Let children especially find love, peace, and protection within our families. We need our families to reflect you in order that our children may grow up in faith. Help us to persevere with family members in patient respect. Help us to show our family members the grace and mercy that you show us. Help us to persist with one another in the way that you have persisted with us. Let the sacrifice and resurrection of your Son stand at the center of our families. Send your Holy Spirit to suffuse our households with your redemption and love. Father, our families need you. They perish for lack of you. We open our arms to you and raise our voices to you that you would come and rescue our families. We call on you to save and restore our families that they may honor, represent, and reflect you. We dedicate our families to you, for you, too, reside in family, Father, Son, and Spirit.

ANSWER

I created you for family. I then instituted your family relationships, husband and wife becoming father and mother to child. I brought forth my own Son within a family. Husband Joseph gave wife Mary to my Spirit to bear my Son, so that father and mother could then raise my Son fulfilling every ancient law and prophecy. Father and mother saved my Son from a murderous king and then raised him to be a strong and well-respected worker. In his youth, My Son obeyed his earthly father and mother, even though he was already King of kings, the universe's ruler. My Son provided for his mother during his time on earth, and when he took to the cross, my Son then gave that provider's role to a friend. I thus not only instituted family for you with the first of men and women but also modeled family for you with my own Son. I want your families to be my families. You will otherwise perish. Only your families can raise children who know me. Only your families can guard the faith. Governments, cultures, and communities may fail you, but you will still survive. When families fail you, you are done. Thus you are right to pray for families. And because you have prayed for families, I will answer your prayer for families while ensuring that your own family raises a child who loves me.

TRANSFORMATION

They had both brought faith to family and also come to faith within family, husband and wife as one. They were each different in background and upbringing, but God devoted them to one another from the moment of their union. God then sanctified their marriage. Though each alone was unholy, they had nevertheless formed a holy union, greater than the sum of two parts and greater surely than either one. Their marriage developed, refined, and matured their faith, teaching them what it meant to be both dutiful and devoted. They learned hard and easy lessons of faith together that they could not have learned alone without the other one. Without each other in a sacramental union, they would have been different, perhaps still devoted to the Lord, but then again perhaps not. Only God would know what might have become of either one of them. They had then raised together a godly child who loved her Lord more than father and mother, proving the holiness of their union. Though father and mother had each done much for their Lord, their child did more for her Lord than either her father or mother, proving the faith of her family. Faith had grown from generation to generation only because they had prayed that God would grant them a faithful family, and God had granted their prayer. God had instituted their marriage as he had instituted the first marriage of Eve to Adam but also the last marriage of Christ to his church, a sacramental union, God in their unity as one.

REVELATION

Family had a special meaning in the kingdom that neither of them had fully or even approximately worked out. The kingdom embraced the fellowship of faith, the bride whom Christ called his church. All residents were as one wed to Christ. While they hadn't understood just what this relationship meant while still on earth, the kingdom made that relationship clear to them. All residents together submitted fully to Christ who simultaneously gave himself to all residents, having cleansed them through his word. The kingdom's residents, unified as one in their affinity to Christ, hewed to Christ as one. Collectively, the residents were, as one, the bride of Christ, in closest relationship. No one resident was more the bride of Christ than another, nor was any one resident the bride of Christ. They were together Christ's bride, his beloved for whom he had given his life. In the kingdom, family had no meaning beyond its divine meaning, just as the divine defined everything else within the kingdom. Thus, they had no worry whether their marriage on earth extended into heaven or how they might relate to their child. Together, they were the same bride and had the same groom in Christ. They were no farther apart in the kingdom than on earth, in fact far closer. They were one as the bride of Christ. This mystery had instant and constant reflection throughout the kingdom. Christ was equally available to all residents in the same relationship because all residents were as one in form of bride to Christ. They each supported one another's immersion in the love of Christ just as they immersed themselves because they were all immersed as one in Christ. No resident competed against another for higher family hierarchy, vaunted family status, or preferred family position. Their family relationship was instead as one with Christ. While they had individual identity to recognize one another, when turning to Christ, they did so not as individuals but as one, as the bride of Christ. The kingdom thus realized all of their earthly prayers to strengthen, unify, preserve, and promote family. The kingdom celebrated but one family, Father, Son, and Spirit, celebrating also the bride of Christ.

Generations

"Your faithfulness continues through all generations." Psalm 119:90.

PRAYER

Father, we pray and petition for generations yet to come. Our concern is not simply for ourselves or even for others sharing this time with us. We also want our children to know and embrace you, and then the children of our children to make the same embrace. We pray that each generation embrace you with greater passion than that which the prior generation had shown. Make our future generations people of strong and working faith. Make their cities shine among the nations like beckoning beacons on hills, drawing others to you. Teach our grandchildren's grandchildren to shout your praise. Cause them to dance in your honor and lift their hands in thanks to your Son. Teach every generation to both know and show your joy. Draw future generations into joining us in your eternal kingdom so that thousands more lift their voices to your glory. Let the heavens resound with their praises and song. Give future generations the courage, discernment, and will to confess, profess, and love you. Father, let us leave for following generations a healthy heritage of faith on which they may draw. Leave no future generation bereft of healthy stock who know and honor you. We care for these future generations just as we care for our own. Let them join you in eternal premises, even as we pray for eternity for our own. Bring future generations into your kingdom so that many more may know your glory and worship you.

ANSWER

Your concern for future generations pleases me. You know that I am the God not only of the past and present but of the future, too. Everyone thinks of their own. Few think of others, and even fewer think of those whom they could not yet even know. Yet I, like you, look down the generations. I see not only the distant past but the future, too. What I do with you may well be to benefit distant future generations. Who but I would know? My foresight is another reason why you should trust me especially when you do not understand my actions. I may be acting now for then, as I acted then for now. You are the beneficiary of the stories and sacrifices of prior generations. Look, even, at my Son who sacrificed for you. If he had hesitated because saving his own life might have been better for his own generation, then think of what he would have lost for yours. No, my Son knew my will. My Son trusted me that I knew how to bring the most out of every generation, for itself and for generations to come. And because you have prayed for future generations rather than only for your own, I will bless your generation while using you to bless future generations even more than I bless your own. You pray as my Son prayed, not for himself but for others, to know and do my will. My will is to do for you while I also do for others, which is why I grant your prayer for future generations, too.

TRANSFORMATION

He had heard others speak of their legacy, which he understood to mean how what they did positively affected future generations. He supposed that he wasn't all that concerned with his own legacy. He expected to be forgotten quite quickly, not just after his natural death but likely even before. Few if any would remember him, surely not after those who knew him in person had also passed on. He didn't want memorials or foundations named after him, didn't want to be famous and in the history books. Yet he did concern himself with a different kind of legacy. He somehow wanted to help ensure that future generations would also know the Lord. He wasn't sure what he could really do for future generations, seeing how difficult he found it to help his own generation in the Lord's knowledge, fear, and love. Yet still, he felt the pull of that possibility. He could help ensure that he and his family loved the Lord and by doing so perhaps help the next generation also know and love the Lord. He might even be able to create something, whether fund or structure or word, that honored the Lord before the next generation and a future generation. If he somehow did so, then he didn't want his name known, only the Lord's name. If he had any reward, then he wanted it to be from the Lord and in the Lord's kingdom. Yet he knew one thing that he could certainly do for future generations, which was to pray to God. And so he prayed that God would pass his Son's grand story and precious faith far into the future, for distant generations.

REVELATION

He had hardly thought in his former life, other for a moment here and there, of one of the great wonders of the kingdom, which was that its residents included all of Christ's generations. He had prayed so earnestly that his own relatives would join him in eternity, and that others whom he knew would also do so, that he had mostly overlooked that salvation was not merely for one's own generation. Generations past were already resident when he arrived, and generations future would soon join him. The kingdom was thus completely unlike earth, which only one's own generation could occupy. Earth's people at any one time represented only a thin slice of humanity that in its total stretched back to the dawn of creation and forward to the end of times. He thought almost entirely of his own generation until he reached the kingdom, where he promptly met and embraced as one all of those whom Christ had saved out of all generations. Salvation was not for just a slice of time. Christ, who was and is, and is to come, is Lord of all generations. God so loved all generations as to send his only Son so that any who would trust in him would receive eternal life. The kingdom thus opened to him a living history that he had just barely imagined. In the kingdom, all ages were real, not just the age out of which each resident had entered. The kingdom's residents, some from millennia ago and others from ages to come, constantly reminded him that it offered eternity, not a slice out of time. The Father indeed was ageless, as was Christ with him, neither bound in culture, history, or time. Christ had entered time at a specific point, as he must have done in order for any to appreciate that he was real. Every follower of Christ also came out of a specific generation, as they must have in order to have chosen to trust in him. Yet those times meant nothing in the kingdom's eternity, where all shared the present time. Christ saved generations as they unfolded, just as he had once prayed. In the kingdom, generations folded back in together out of eternal time.

Leaders

"Remember your leaders, who spoke God's word to you." Hebrews 13:7.

PRAYER

We pray for our leaders, Father, that they may know and follow you. We pray that our leaders may discern and do your will for us whom they serve. We know the great challenge of leadership, which is to set aside selfish interests in favor of our interests, the interests of those whom leaders serve. Without your Spirit, selfish leaders seek and acquire power to preserve their own privilege and position. Without your word, selfish leaders sacrifice us, whom God appointed them to serve. Yet under your Spirit and word, sound leaders serve selflessly and sacrificially in broad interest of their people. Give us these selfless, servant leaders, Father. Make selfless and effective at service our current leaders. Strengthen them not for their own cause but for the cause of those whom they govern. Give them courage not for their own pursuits but for our interests as the people whom they serve. Give them the heart of your Son, oh Father, who gave everything that all whom he served might embrace you. Help our leaders pursue and find you, Father, and in doing so find the wisdom that they need to lead. Help us to find and follow those leaders who have your heart and exercise your wisdom. We need your leadership, Father, and so we pray that your Spirit would inhabit and work through our leaders, guiding them in your holy path. Under your godly leaders, then let us rise up as a people not solely in commerce or military power but in your holy and righteous way. Help our leaders help us to be a godly nation and people. Teach our leaders your righteous way. And if they do not learn, then replace them swiftly with leaders who do know and follow your way.

Answer

Because I am sovereign and rule above all, I also institute and appoint authority. Your leaders lead because I give them that mantle. My giving them the mantle of leadership does not mean that they will lead in my Spirit, in my righteous way. My leadership is servant leadership, as my Son led to serve all. Your leaders seldom lead in my servant way. They far too often lead for themselves rather than for you and your fellow citizens. They far too often lead for their own honor, preening and praising their virtues when they are utterly corrupt. When they lead in their own way, rejecting my servant Son, then your people, communities, and nation suffer. Without me, your leaders promote wanton killing of the weak and defenseless. They steal from future generations to ensure the comfort of their own. They dishonor the past, corrupt the present, and destroy the future, all to ensure that they remain in power. Yet when they turn back to me and lead in my righteous way and for my honor, then your people, communities, and nation rise. The strong then work diligently not only for themselves but also for others. The weak then once again find protection. Families once again grow fruitful and strong. You are right to look and pray for godly leaders who sacrifice their own interests for the interests of their communities and the nation, that all may do likewise for the good of all. And so I answer your prayer. Your corrupt leaders will fall with your nation and communities, while I raise up new leaders of my own.

Transformation

Other generations, like his own, had also lived through fear of their corrupt and godless leaders, seeing the nation and communities become corrupt with them and fall. His generation had realized the awful consequences in death, fear, and misery that its corrupt leaders imposed. Under its corrupt leaders, his generation had seen millions slaughtered and many more enslaved. His generation's leaders had stolen vast amounts of wealth that the next generation would have to pay while promising his generation vast amounts more than the next generation could possibly pay. His generation's commerce had pitted capital against labor and labor against capital, creating warring rather than cooperating estates. His generation's military withdrew from its peacekeeping role, resulting in the genocide of God's own followers. His generation's policies had decimated families and divided communities. Godless governing elites sheltered themselves from common citizens while sneering at their citizens' odor. Yet other generations, like his own, had also seen godly, servant leaders who sacrificed their own interests and legacies for the good of those whom they governed, for the good of all. His generation had seen godly leaders who warned against the slaughter of its own innocents, theft from future generations, and other deep corruptions. His generation thus knew the value of godly leaders over corrupt leaders. The question his generation thus posed was how God could possibly bless a nation and people whose godless leaders his generation had let draw the nation so far down corruption's awful path.

REVELATION

The kingdom of course had but a single leader, as he so well knew and appreciated. Gone were the old confused days of having many leaders, most of them moving in their own direction. All kingdom residents looked to God whom they obeyed gladly for his divine direction. The kingdom's population moved in unison around the loving dictates of the most generous God. What surprised him, though, was that the kingdom still evidenced forms of subsidiary leadership, not alternative leadership as had been the case on earth, with everyone going in their own direction, but residents who, in following the perfect mandates of the glorious God, led others to also do so. Indeed, every kingdom resident had abundant leadership opportunities. He noticed how frequently he followed the actions of others, knowing that anyone who led did so under a special discernment of the will of God. Grand assemblies for worship occurred as if spontaneously but in fact led by residents who had discerned the specific will of God. Leaders led just as God directed, and followers followed gladly knowing that as followers they pursued the unseen will of God. Even more to his surprise, he, too, led others when at times he discerned God's specific desire in ways not seen by others who followed him. Thus, great movements occurred throughout the kingdom in perfect order, all of which celebrated God. The greatest of these movements involved God's glorious worship. Leaders bore no burden, facing no conflict between their own intentions and those of their divine Creator, and no dissension among resident ranks. Under such consonant leadership, the kingdom pulsed with God's glorious harmonies.

Workers

"'I am a fellow servant with you, holding to Jesus.'" Revelation 19:10.

PRAYER

Father, we pray for fellow workers. We pray for those trusted friends who labor alongside us in your fields and vineyards. We work together connected to you so that you make your good things grow for harvest. First protect these fellow workers, Father, for whom you planned good works. Do not let evil tempt them away from their assigned good work or from you. Hold them close to you. Guard them not only from evil but also from themselves, against the deception of their hearts. Keep them instead turned toward you in whom they find both their ministry and salvation. Then strengthen them. Yes, make them effective, creative, and productive. Guide them so that through their willing effort you supply a bounty of blessing. More so, give them the energy and vitality to carry your word into the world for a harvest of souls. Equip them so that your word that they carry would bring others out of the world to you. Fill them with your word, and then help them to spread that word across the lives and paths of others. Help them to serve in your name until those others join them in your service. Give our fellow workers the wisdom and discernment to see your path and to show it to others. Give them knowledge of your word and the courage to share it with others. Help them project your Son's image into the world as a beacon of hope. Help them that they may point others to your Son in order that those others may also enter your kingdom. Form our fellow workers into faithful fellowship so that they may encourage one another and in doing so encourage others to join them in your work. We pray for our fellow workers, Father, knowing that you answer this prayer that we make in your Son's name and in your will.

ANSWER

You are my worker tilling and preparing to harvest my fields, those which I have sown. You are right to pray for more workers because I have told you that the harvest is plentiful but that workers are few. Go find me more workers. Tell them to help you spread my good news.

Make workers of your family, friends, and acquaintances. Help them join you in my great commission. Help them fish not for sport or sustenance but for persons. Show them how I send out workers. Show them what you do in working in my fields. Invite them to join you in those fields, and then teach them to spread my good news. I want many more workers joining you. When I say that the harvest is plentiful, I mean that many would love and obey my Son if only someone told them of him. When I say that the workers are few, I mean that too few speak of my Son to others who need to hear of him. Many know and obey my Son but do little or nothing to help others join them. Do not be selfish about eternal life. My kingdom was not made solely for you. My kingdom has room for all who wish to enter it, all who wish to join you. And because you have prayed for fellow workers in my fields, I will put workers before you for you to recruit for bringing in the harvest. No one who helps reap a rich harvest will go without reward. All who harvest will receive their full reward in heaven. Don't you want my heavenly reward? Your reward in heaven will be greater than anything that you can gain on earth, if you will only recruit workers to help you bring in the harvest.

Transformation

She felt that she was still learning to be an evangelist. She sensed that she could be much bolder, that she was letting slip away opportunities to speak of her Lord to others who did not know him. Even as she turned her heart and mind to learning how to be a better evangelist, though, she also realized that she could do a better job of having others join her in the harvest. She hadn't thought before that she should ask others to help her. She had always seen evangelism as an individual thing. But then she remembered that Christ had sent out workers two by two. Maybe she shouldn't be doing everything on her own. Maybe she should be asking her family and friends to join her in telling others about their Lord and Savior. She realized that in all of her prayers for the Lord to make her an evangelist, she could also pray that he would make evangelists of those other followers whom she knew and with whom she might work for the harvest. She saw that her community of followers had hardly begun to bring in the harvest. She saw, too, that the harvest was plentiful, just as Christ had said. She wanted the heavenly reward for bringing in a rich harvest. Indeed, she wanted that reward not just for herself but for her family and friends, too. God, she prayed, help my follower friends join me in your great commission to reap a rich harvest.

Revelation

She had anticipated that she would have completed her work by the time that she entered the kingdom, and so it was. The work of the loving God was to harvest souls into eternal glory with God. God had so loved the world that he sacrificed his only Son that whoever then trusted the Son would live eternally with the Son and Father. God did not seek to chastise but to love, as his Son's painful sacrifice proved beyond cavil. She had in her former life told her family, friends, and acquaintances of that great truth that everyone had the choice of living with the loving God forever or of perishing apart from him. She had tried to show everyone the love of God. Her labor in doing so had been intermittent, halting, and timid, as were the labors of other workers in the rich harvest fields. Yet she had nonetheless pursued the work with some degree of diligence, anticipating its promised kingdom reward. Once in the kingdom, she knew that her harvesting was over because every resident had been a follower of Christ and pursuer of the loving God. Her witness was no longer to the uninformed who needed first the knowledge and then the love to know that she spoke of the one true God. Her kingdom witness, like the witness of every other kingdom resident, was simply to God's glory. They all knew and had already navigated the sure path through Christ to that loving God. She was no longer a harvester. Whatever harvest she had reaped was there before her as her reward among the celebrating residents. And what a rich, rich reward it was.

Teachers

"In your teaching show integrity, seriousness, and soundness." Titus 2:7.

Prayer

Father, we pray for teachers. We pray for those whom you and your people entrust to share your word and truth. We pray for wise teachers to help us explore, examine, and investigate your history and prophecy fulfilled. We pray that our teachers would then nurture conviction in the faith grounded on the real and reliable. Make our teachers sage while keeping them authentic. We know that our teachers cannot learn and share truth without involving themselves in acts of knowing, those acts illustrating your word while proving their faith. So help our teachers not just preach but also live your word, much as your Son became the word and truth in form corporeal. Although he was God divine, your Son took on earthly flesh, humbly human form, so that we could see and therefore know the truth. In similar way, help our teachers not just to talk but to take stances of knowing and knowledge. Prove them convicted by your truth to share your truth with those whom they lead in learning. Give our teachers pure hearts, clear minds, and your Holy Spirit. Give them the will to love and care for others deeply, even sacrificially, as your Son loved and cared. Do not let anyone lead our teachers astray. Do not let them languish without student. Push, pull, and compel them onward, forward, and upward toward you, growing in wise action and sound knowledge. Father, we pray that our teachers take on the image of your Son who taught so profoundly, always pointing to you. Give our teachers your wisdom and the persistence, patience, and heart of your glorious Son. We lose our way without sound teachers.

ANSWER

You need teachers who know me and devote themselves to me. You need these teachers to remind you of my word. My Spirit reveals my word to you, just as teachers whom my Spirit fills reveal my word to you. Without teachers who know my word and have my Spirit, you too easily follow blind guides. Blind guides lead you to destruction. My teachers, those whom my Spirit fills, lead you to eternal life. Seek out teachers whose fruit proves them trustworthy. Avoid teachers whose actions deny their words. You will know my teachers, those whom my Spirit fills, by their fruit. You will know them by what their students learn from them and do under them. When you see their students speaking and doing right, then you will know that my Spirit fills them. When you see their students speaking and doing wrong, then you will know to avoid them. Do not follow blind guides. Follow teachers who produce good fruit. Pray for your teachers often. They are that important to you. Pray that they learn ever more of me and from my Spirit. The more that your teachers learn of me and from my Spirit, the more that you, too, will learn from them. No two walk together but that they share a common wisdom. Do not follow those who do not know my word. Learn only from teachers who know and trust my word, and who love me. And because you have prayed for your teachers, I will show you on whom to rely. I will give you my Spirit's discernment for wise guides. Beyond granting your prayer for sound teachers, I will also make you a teacher of my word, ensuring that you carry my Spirit. Those who learn deeply from wise teachers learn enough to teach.

TRANSFORMATION

He loved instruction. He had been a lifelong student but only recently a teacher, and even then not expressly a teacher of God's word, only a teacher of faith in a secular institution. Yet as much as he loved instruction, he had over the years found that he only loved instruction that held God's word. Instruction, wherever he found it, either respected or did not respect God's word. Sometimes distinguishing the instruction, godly from ungodly, took a little more discernment. Sometimes distinguishing sound from unsound instruction even took some evidence of the teacher's actions rather than just the teacher's words. But soon, with most instruction, he could discern its foundation, whether working for the kingdom or against it. His increasing discernment helped him ensure that his own instruction, even within a secular rather than sacred institution, respected God's word. He also wanted to ensure that he had so much of God's Spirit in him as to continue to do God's good works including sharing the good news of God's Son. Then, if anyone looked behind his instruction to his fruit, as he sometimes did with other instructors, he hoped that they would see fruit of God's Spirit. He had never cared to learn just for learning's sake. He would also never want to teach just for teaching's sake. All activity was for the glory of God, both learning and teaching.

REVELATION

While the kernel of his former life had been one of learning and teaching the word God, the kingdom offered its residents a different kind of instruction. All kingdom residents already knew and embraced the passionate glory of Christ's cross. Every kingdom resident had much yet to learn of the depth and expressions of that passion. God loved the kingdom's residents in ways that every resident had much to learn. He was relieved and pleased to discover that God provided teachers and aids in that instruction. Every resident had both a learning and teaching ministry, to learn new glories of God while showing those glories to others in order that every resident grow in the honor of God. If he had thought enough about the question, then he would have assumed that those who entered heaven did so in perfect state and thus never to grow and learn for the better. He would have been wrong. While every resident indeed entered the kingdom washed of all sin and corruption, every resident also entered with little clear knowledge of the many glorious things of God. God's kingdom is a mystery to all on earth, one that the scriptures reveal only in part. To embrace the new realm in resurrected life requires vast learning, for which he needed and benefitted from much instruction. God's teachers and aids were exceedingly kind to him, helping him make many profound adjustments. He might have remained lost without them. In time, he assumed his own role in introducing new residents to the kingdom's glories. God, who had blessed him with an earthly teaching ministry, granted him a glorious kingdom reprise of his former teacher's role.

Students

"Everyone fully trained is like their teacher." Luke 6:40.

PRAYER

Father, we pray for students. We pray for those young and old who are learning new knowledge, wisdom, and skills with which they may serve you. We pray that others may learn how to do your good works, supply your protection, and serve your justice. We pray that students would learn how to provide your comfort, care, and healing. We need these new capacities, Father, to do as you would have us do with the time and talents that you have given us. We do not want to enter your eternal kingdom before we have completed the work that you have for us to do here. To do your will, we need to learn new ways for our old habits. We need to discover new applications of old truths. We need to understand, appreciate, and respect others. We also need to learn to support ourselves, our families, and others. We further need to learn to teach and guide others, each of whom you made in your image. We must learn and know in order to care. We must have skill in order to serve. You brought us into the world barely formed, Father, with so much to learn. We must grow so much wiser before we can do as you wish and admonish. We can accomplish so little of your will without first being good students. Make us good students not only of the world but especially of your word and Son, guided by your Holy Spirit. Inspire students to engage fully in study of your word and your kingdom ways in this world. Lead students to engage the world for you and your glorious Son. Give us the ear, mind, and heart to discern, to see, grasp, and grow. Help us to learn continually, at all ages, in all stages. Make us larger vessels, Father, for the Spirit of your Son. Help us, we pray, to learn.

ANSWER

You are my student. I am your teacher. I created you with great capacity to learn. I could have filled you with skill and knowledge. Yet if I had done so on my own, done your learning for you, then you would not have grown strong and mature through your discipline and in struggles. I want you to learn to discipline yourself. I want you to push yourself through subjects that you do not know until they reveal themselves to you. You will only make an effective witness for me if you involve yourself in your own learning. You are not a sponge soaking up knowledge. You are not a container into which I can pour my word. I made you human, in my image. I made you to act on your ambition, to feel the fire of my word within you. I wanted my word to crush all laziness and languor within you. I wanted you to struggle and scrap to know me and then to go into battle for my word. Only by making you strong through your own initiative tested against my challenges could I use you. My great commission does not rely on the weak and timid but on the strong and courageous. I love boldness and confidence in my students, just as I love boldness and confidence in my teachers. And because you have prayed for students, that you and others would continue to learn, I grant your prayer. I will keep the fire to learn burning within you. Moreover, you will learn things that you can put into use in carrying out my great commission. Learn, my child. You are my student.

TRANSFORMATION

She finally figured that she was never going to stop learning, particularly about God's word. Probably, earlier in life, she had a vague sense that one could know what one needed from the Bible, know enough about the faith. At times, earlier in life, she had even believed that she was nearing that point of sufficient knowledge. Yet whenever she approached what she thought might be full-enough learning, the point when she could relax in her studies, the point seemed quickly to recede into the distance. The further that she advanced, the more distant her endpoint seemed to be. She gradually realized that she was learning that God's word was inexhaustible. It contained riches beyond understanding. The more that she learned of God's word, the more that she knew that she had yet more to learn. God's word expanded with her learning rather than contracted. Horizons opened up farther with every revelation of God's word, rather than approaching nearer. God's kingdom grew larger, richer, and yet more unknowable than ever, with every little thing that she learned, rather than looking smaller and more clearly bounded and defined. She could even look back at the times that she had thought that she was nearing sufficient knowledge, and see that she was actually then not learning. Those had been the times when her eyes had been looking away from God rather than more closely at him, and her mind had been closing rather than opening. She finally learned to pray not that God would show her everything that she needed to know but that God would make her his student so that she could continue to learn forever. She prayed the same thing for others.

REVELATION

To her delight, the kingdom gave her endless opportunities to introduce new residents to the wonders of God. She had been an earnest student in her former life, soaking up the word of God in its many special expressions. She had been an equally earnest student, indeed far more so, when she first entered the kingdom. Its wonders, each of them pointing out the glory of God, enthralled her. She had wanted to know and see more of them in order that she could know better her loving God. While the wonders never ceased, she gradually acquired sufficient knowledge of enough of them that she found herself naturally introducing them to newer residents. An earnest student in her own right, she could now share the kingdom's special splendors with each new resident whom she encountered so that together they could witness and marvel at more of the glories of God. She loved being a student of her Lord, in effect sitting at his feet while he showed her ever greater wonders, revealing the mysteries of God. Her Lord helped her understand that God didn't want to remain a continual mystery but instead wanted to reveal himself in ways that his students could learn and appreciate. God wanted to be their intimate, familiar Lord in human image even if divine form, not merely a distant spectral marvel. He could not gain that proximity and familiarity without the kingdom's residents being avid students of his character and ways. The kingdom was one great classroom for the loving wonders of the almighty God. She wanted everyone to grow and share in her love for learning about the Lord. He had welcomed her as his student, ready to share with her all that she could hold in her knowledge of God.

Lost

"The Son of Man came to save the lost." Luke 19:10.

PRAYER

Above all, Father, we pray and petition for lost souls. We pray for those who do not yet know you. We also pray for those who, though knowing of you, have not yet accepted your Son as their only path back to you. We pray for those who do not yet know of your kingdom. We pray for those who do not yet know that you offer them eternal life. These lost souls are not strangers or enemies. These lost souls are our mothers and fathers, brothers and sisters, sons and daughters. They are our neighbors, co-workers, and friends. Father, we care so deeply about these lost souls as to bring their need for your salvation constantly before you. We also pray for the salvation of people whom we have never met, even generations not yet born. Help these souls see your light, Father, so that you may draw them to you. Break down the barriers that they erect against you, while also breaking the barriers that others erect against them. Frustrate their wayward ways, while opening before them your narrow but sure path. Open before them your Son's path of the cross, which would open their path to you. Show them your holiness and righteousness. Show them also your love, magnificence, and power. Show them that you are everything that they desire, everything that they pursue. And help us also to be your light to them, Father. Help us to do our part as your Holy Spirit moves within and through us. Give us the love and courage, the sensitivity and generosity, to welcome and move them. Help us to awaken them from the slumber that will be their death and eternal loss of you. Father, bring these lost souls back to you.

ANSWER

My concern is for the lost. I leave ninety-nine saved souls to rescue the hundredth soul who is lost. I am the savior God, the one whose heart is for the lost. My sacrificing my Son for the lost shows you that I care infinitely for the lost. My love for the lost has no bounds. I do not withhold salvation from anyone. I have given all that I have that all would have eternal life. All that my lost souls lack is someone to tell them how to find me. If you tell them the good news that they have me, their one great and true God, if they want me, then they will have all that they need to know. Their salvation will be theirs if they choose it. You are right to pray for lost souls. Your prayer pursues my own heart. You are right to pray that I would send my followers to them. You are right to pray that when my followers have told them the good news, that their hearts would turn to me. I have answered your prayers. I am sending workers into the harvest fields for the many lost souls. I am also calling to those who have heard the good news but not yet responded to me. I am showing them more of my glory, the glory that I gave to my Son whom I sent for them. My Spirit is at work, too, moving my followers to love those who have heard the good news but not yet responded. And because you have prayed pursuing my own heart for lost souls, I will give you a rich harvest of lost souls, your reward for which will await you in heaven. Bring in the harvest, for the fields are ripe and bountiful.

TRANSFORMATION

He couldn't quite explain it, but every day seemed to bring him greater heart for lost souls. Every day seemed to bring him greater desire to carry word of Jesus to them. Much of his life had been looking for the Lord. Another large part of it had been learning more about the Lord whom he found. Although he hadn't really planned or expected it, he seemed now to have reached that point in his life where his greatest concern was for others. His concern was even for those whom he did not yet know or may never know. The reason for this change in his outlook may have been that God had finally turned the heart of his own father who until his deathbed had resisted the Lord's earnest rescue. He had long prayed for his father's miracle salvation, that salvation which his father had firmly rejected right up to within hours of his death. God's miraculous answer to his prayer confirmed his faith in God and in prayers for salvation. And so he had begun to pray more often for salvation for others beyond his own family and acquaintances. He began also to pray for the heart, mind, skill, and discernment to share the good news that would save all if only all had the desire for it. God just seemed again to be answering his prayers. God was giving him a greater heart for the lost, just like God's own heart. God was also giving him the Spirit's discernment and courage. God had many more to save in rich harvest of bountiful fields. He expected to be a part of it.

REVELATION

He knew that the kingdom was for the saved, not for the lost. Indeed, every resident whom he met had accepted the same assurance that he had embraced. Christ was their only means of entry. He could only imagine the numbers who had not made that embrace. The kingdom welcomed many residents from all nations and lands. Yet he imagined that for every resident that the kingdom welcomed, another had refused Christ's embrace, which was their choice. On earth, he would have felt great sadness over their loss. He would have taken that emotion as another spur to love and reach out to those lost while they still had time to make their eternal election. In the kingdom, though, he could only celebrate those who had relied on Christ as their one and only Savior. God denies no one the choice. He instead gives each the freedom to accept or reject his passionate love. Love has no other choice. The kingdom would forever remain a witness to his love and glory, not a warning to those who had made another choice. He trusted that God had done as God must do to give each the best of him. Those who did not join him in the kingdom had chosen not to live eternally with God, which was their right. He only thanked God that he had an opportunity in his former life to be his witness, even if he also knew that he had done it too seldom and poorly. God in his fathomless love had saved him even from his greatest shortcoming in not praying more often and working more earnestly to bring home another lost.

Epilogue

"The Lord answers according to a person's motives." Proverbs 16:1.

Father, you know our prayers. We know that we need say nothing and that you would know our hearts without a word said. Your Spirit would utter groans for us that our words could not express, and you would hear and answer that utterance because you cannot silence your own voice nor deny yourself. You would grant the wishes of your Son who wishes nothing other than your will being done. Still, we turn to you in prayer because to commune with you is our need. We need to speak with you, just as we need to hear from you. We have recorded here your answers to our prayers, fearing error in doing so, because only you know. Yet every prayer that we make to you presumes that we know something of which prayers you would answer. You say that you do not answer because we pray with wrong motives, and so we examine our motives to see if they please you. In doing so, we presume to know what pleases you, indeed, which prayers you would answer. And so we hope and pray that our recording your answers is not any too greater of a presumption than is prayer itself. If all prayer presumes knowledge of your will, then all prayer presumes that we know something of your answer. Thus, Father, accept not only our prayers but our record of your answers. We pray, knowing that you hear and knowing how reliable is your answer.

Index of Prayers

Abandoned	292
Adoration	5
Anger	67
Beauty	102
Blessing	89
Carnality	77
Communication	131
Confession	45
Creation	19
Creativity	21
Deceit	75
Discipline	94
Divinity	34
Doubt	45
Eternity	31
Families	141
Father	5
Fear	54
Fellowship	109
Generations	144
Glory	51
Greed	14
Healing	136
Heart	139
Idolatry	83
Impatience	17
Ingratitude	59
Intimacy	24
Judgment	70
Justice	134
Leaders	147
Life	107
Locality	42
Lost	157
Lust	24
Love	16

Motives	48
Prayer	29
Pride	62
Protection	129
Provision	124
Redemption	112
Relationship	86
Rest	120
Resurrection	115
Secrecy	72
Service	99
Shelter	126
Sloth	56
Son	8
Sovereignty	39
Spirit	11
Students	155
Superiority	80
Supplication	123
Teachers	152
Thanksgiving	86
Trials	96
Truth	117
Vocation	104
Word	14
Workers	149
Worship	26

www.ingramcontent.com/pod-product-compliance
Lightning Source LLC
Chambersburg PA
CBHW070617300426
44113CB00010B/1562